What I Learned from God While...

QUILTING

What I Learned from God While...
QUILTING

Ruth McHaney Danner
&
Cristine Bolley

PROMISE
PRESS
An Imprint of Barbour Publishing

Published by Promise Press, an imprint of Barbour Publishing, Inc., P.O. Box 719, Uhrichsville, Ohio 44683 http://www.barbourbooks.com

Member of the
Evangelical Christian
Publishers Association

Printed in the United States of America.

Dedication

To the memory of
my mother, Kate McHaney,
to grandmothers Clare Lowry and Grace McHaney,
to all master quilters who instilled in me
a love of quilting,
and to all the quilters
who have used their hands to serve others,
and to all those who
appreciate the gift of a quilt.

I will open my mouth in parables,
I will utter hidden things, things from of old—
what we have heard and known,
what our fathers have told us.
We will not hide them from their children;
we will tell the next generation
the praiseworthy deeds of the LORD,
his power, and the wonders he has done."
PSALM 78:2–4

Contents

$\mathcal{A}$ $\mathcal{N}$ote from Cristine

I was four the first time I asked God for understanding and ten when I asked Him for wisdom. In my early conversations with God I talked but never listened for answers. I was a teenager when I discovered the Scripture that says, "God looks down from heaven on the sons of men to see if there are any who understand, any who seek God" (Psalm 53:2). I especially remember the day I read Jeremiah 29:13 which says, "You will seek me and find me when you seek me with all your heart."

So, I began looking harder for God. The more I looked the more I understood that it is easy to find Him. He is always near, eager to reveal His purpose, plan, provision, power, and consequential peace. God is always quick to answer when I ask Him what He thinks of my plans. Sometimes He speaks through people, sometimes through circumstances too perfect to be coincidental, and more often of late, He speaks through a still small voice somewhere within my thoughts. But in all cases, when it is truly His voice, a word can be found in the Bible to support His answer.

Many times I have read the books in the Bible by Matthew, Mark, Luke, and John. All of these men lived with and listened to Jesus. Through their four accounts, I could watch what Jesus did and hear what He said. Jesus did not teach religious rituals but spoke of a relationship with God, compelling His audience to ask their Father in heaven for whatever was needed.

It is wise to listen to Jesus. Matthew said in chapter 13 (v. 34) that Jesus never taught anything without a short story that illustrated a moral attitude or spiritual principle, otherwise known as a parable, thereby fulfilling the prophecy of Psalm 78:2. He used familiar visual aids, such as seeds and birds, to illustrate the wonders of God and the certainty of His participation in our lives.

Jesus showed us that nothing can separate us from the love of God, because He is ever present, pursuing us through our hobbies, our work, our relationships, and our solitude. I now expect to see biblical truths in every facet of personal experience, and I have never found God to be silent when I have asked Him for wisdom. So this time I asked Him to show me what I could learn from a quilt, and the idea of this book began to take root.

I met Ruth Danner through a mutual friend, Niki Anderson, who was already working with me on parables from her gardening experiences. I asked Ruth to tell me stories about quilters she had met through the years. With what seemed to be effortless speed, she returned this collection of heartwarming anecdotes to me.

I've never completed a quilt, but I have learned valuable lessons through the four quilts that have touched my life. My husband, James, surprised me one day by suggesting that we make a quilt together. We were newlyweds living in New Zealand with a three-year work visa and no television. We started the project with great enthusiasm.

We made a cardboard template and cut countless hexagons from our old jeans and cotton prints left over from the dresses I had made. Many cold winter evenings we worked together, sitting side-by-side and as close as we could get to the one electric panel heater that we owned.

Occasionally we switched places with each other to warm the sides of our faces that had been away from the heat. We talked of future goals as we hand-stitched the hexagons together. However, we soon became busy with new friends and put away the pieces. Over the past thirty years, we have often talked about finishing the quilt. Today we understand that we were learning how make our dreams come true, one patient stitch at a time.

My first comforter was from my grandmother. It was made with squares of wool from my grandfather's suits, pieced with heavy black velvet, and tied with pink yarn. My college roommate took it with her on a trip. On her way home, she had an accident, and though she was not hurt, her car was totaled and towed to a salvage yard in another city. She didn't think to get the quilt out of her trunk before it was taken away. By the time we called the keeper of the salvage yard, someone had already taken it.

The loss of that comforter and its connection to my beloved

grandparents grieved me. Though I should have been happy that my roommate was all right, I only felt frustration over her negligence. When she offered to pay me one hundred dollars (a considerable amount at that time) from her insurance settlement, I accepted the money without thanking her.

Years later, after hearing a sermon on restitution, I prayed, *Lord, show me if I've ever taken something from someone that I should return.* In an instant, the memory of accepting her money came to mind. Once I learned her new address I mailed a check and an apology for not being more concerned about her needs at the time of the accident. I realized she could have used the money for replacing her car, but I selfishly had accepted payment for something that had been given freely to me. I mentioned in my apology that I believed God had told me to return the money. I wondered what she would think about that since she had never expressed an interest in a personal relationship with Him when we were roommates.

She wrote back a gracious thank you letter, stating that the money arrived at a desperate time for her. She had just prayed, *God, where can I get the money that I need?* I learned that day that I still had the best part of my grandparents, whose clothes had been made into the comforter; I had found their joy of giving which they had exemplified throughout their lives.

A four-patch quilt that my husband's grandmother made was given to us by my mother-in-law when we returned from New

Zealand. The quilt was quite old and though I was young, I understood its value and respected the hours of work it represented. In the winter, I sometimes display it over the banister at the top of our stairs, where it is the focal point for all who enter our home. By looking at the tiny stitches, we are reminded that work done well will remain and cause our children's children to remember us.

My favorite quilt is bright purple and yellow with large rings made from patches of wild, multi-colored prints that I would not have imagined putting together. The interlocking rings form playful visual exchanges of circles or flowers, depending on how your eyes focus on the pattern.

I bought this purple quilt at an antique store several years ago for forty dollars. Some of the stitches are loose, and some of the fabric is worn so thin that you can see the muslin backing from the front. But the best thing about my purple quilt is we're not afraid to use it. It's the quilt we grab when we go on picnics, sit in front of the fire, or throw on the patio table to decorate for a spring tea party.

My spiritual growth can be told in the four quilts I have owned, from seeking comfort, to seeking a future, to collecting old valuable treasures, and finally to finding great pleasure from imperfect, practical, and useable things. My faith served me well during those times of longing, planning, acquiring, and now simply living.

I have matured with the quilts. I no longer react as selfishly as I did when my grandmother's comforter was lost. The New Zealand quilt taught me how to make my own comfort. The four-patch quilt opened my eyes to the value of others who have worked to make us comfortable. And like the purple quilt, I am at peace with my imperfect, but colorful faith. God has kept His promise to never forsake me, even when my faith was thin and pulling loose.

The prophet Isaiah spoke of God in chapter 26 (v. 3) of his book, saying, "You will keep in perfect peace him whose mind is steadfast, because he trusts in you." As you, the reader, enjoy the following stories, keep your mind on God and snuggle into the comfort He can give you through a quilt.

CRISTINE BOLLEY

Acknowledgments

Thanks to all the quilters I met on-line and in person, whose stories I have written here. Their willing assistance and gracious encouragement were key factors in the completion of this book.

Thanks to my husband, Mark Danner, whose patient instruction in the realm of computers saved me untold hours of grief on this project.

A special thanks to fellow author Niki Anderson for her valuable critiquing throughout the writing process, and for her introducing me to co-author Cristine Bolley.

Thanks to Cristine's husband, James, who spent late nights discussing my stories with her, and who contributed godly insights to many of "The Quilting Frame" lessons.

And to Susan Schlabach and Barbour Publishing, Inc. for pursuing the parables found in the life experiences of a quilter.

A Note from Ruth

A patchwork quilt evokes images of warmth, home, and comfort. Born of the need for serviceable bedcovers, the quilt is utilitarian as well as attractive. It thereby offers physical, emotional, and even spiritual comfort. Interestingly, such comfort can come in the making of the quilt, or in the giving of it, or in the receiving of it. As you read these true stories, you may come to realize that the ultimate Giver of comfort is God Himself, Who sometimes offers His comfort through human hands holding needles and thread and scissors and fabric.

Each story is an individual unit, complete within itself. Each is more than just a story, however. You'll want to look at "The Quilting Frame" at the end of every vignette to give you something to ponder when applying a quilting experience to a deeper truth. A quilt frame, after all, is the structural foundation of our craft.

"God's Template" gives a Bible verse pointing to the heart of the story. A quilter's templates are the patterns we use when cutting pieces or marking quilting lines. We trust that their angles and dimensions are correct.

Read "The Binding Stitch" for a prayerful thought relating to the story. One of the final steps in quilting is the binding. This gives the quilt its finished look and makes it complete. Without the binding, the quilt wouldn't be fit to face the world.

Finally, you'll find interesting and helpful quilting tips in each "Scrap Bag." These ideas come from my years at the sewing machine and quilting frame. They may offer you a time- or labor-saving idea, an accident-prevention method, or a new twist on a traditional quilting procedure.

RUTH MCHANEY DANNER

The Quilting Frame

A local bank invited me to set up a quilting demonstration in their lobby. The day of the show was scheduled to coincide with our town's pioneer celebration. All kinds of nearly-forgotten skills were on display throughout the town: shoeing horses in the city park, making butter at the supermarket, milking cows by hand on the courthouse lawn.

I arrived that morning before the bank was open, and a security guard let me in. In about ten minutes, I set up my PVC floor frame and stretched my quilt across it. The bank provided portable room dividers for me to display other quilts as well. While I hung them, I considered the special memories that these works represented.

I thought of the days I had spent quilting at a community education center. Smoothing out my friendship quilt, I remembered showing the craft to a new friend from Japan. Finally, as I arranged the Grandmother's Flower Garden quilt, I imagined Grandma enjoying peaceful days at her quilting frame.

By the time the bank unlocked the doors I was ready for the crowd, armed with needle, thread, and thimble. Hour after hour, people of all ages came to see my quilts. As they walked in the door, their eyes focused on my work in progress, a multi-colored Dresden plate pattern on a soft pink background.

To my amusement, the people's reactions differed, usually depending on their ages. Children often clung to their mothers with one hand and stroked the quilt with the other. They sometimes said a word or two about the "big blanket" or "pretty colors."

Teenagers, by contrast, asked questions. "Hey, isn't this the same stuff my grandma likes to make?"

"My great-aunt Rachel quilted me one when I graduated from high school. Do you think it took her a long time?"

"How can you stand to do such slow work?"

Older adults inquired about my PVC frame. "It wasn't like that when I was a young 'un. How'd you get this quilt on here, anyway?"

"Did you set this thing up all by yourself?"

"Yep, I remember Mama's quiltin' frame. Hung down from the ceiling. Did ya ever see one of those? Now, *that's* a real frame!"

One older gentleman reminded me of my father. "There was a lot of sisters in my family," he said, "and a'course they could all quilt. Every evenin' after supper—except Sunday—Mama and the girls would clear up the dishes, wash 'em, and sweep the floor. Then, they'd lower that quiltin' frame, which hung above the dinin' table. Spent a couple hours before bedtime, workin' on the quilt. Us boys'd be cleanin' the huntin' rifles, or greasin' our boots. Them was good times for us!"

I smiled in agreement, thinking, *Yes, quilting gives us much more than quilts.* I added this day at the bank to my list of treasured memories.

The Quilting Frame: People see different things when they look at my quilts. Some enjoy the warmth of the fabric without considering my talent, some are impressed with the time I have spent. Surprisingly, some are more interested in the frame than in the quilt itself. The framework is a vital part of my labor, as is the moral framework of our lives. If I use a faulty frame, the tension of my threads varies, and the resulting quilt will be less than perfect.

God's Template: "He has showed you, O man, what is good. And what does the LORD require of you? To act justly and to love mercy and to walk humbly with your God" (Micah 6:8).

The Binding Stitch: Lord, keep me on Your framework, so my work is not in vain.

Scrap Bag: Post a sign at your quilting demonstrations that says, *Please do not touch the quilts.* Or, provide clean gloves for observers to wear when handling your quilts. Remember not to touch your face before touching a quilt, since make-up can leave a permanent mark on the fabric.

Block-of-the-Month

A few years ago, in a Texas quilt guild, two women faced a similar problem with different solutions.

Alice and Rita were precision piecers and excellent quilters. They each made two or three full-size quilts a year, machine pieced and hand-quilted. Their work earned ribbons in county fairs and quilt shows throughout the area.

At each meeting, their quilt guild sponsored a block-of-the-month drawing. Any interested member would purchase a pattern and fabric kit for a small fee and make the block. The next month all participants would bring their blocks and enter their names in a drawing. The lucky winner would take home enough blocks for a quilt top.

Alice and Rita always made a block-of-the-month. Each of their efforts was beautifully, accurately pieced, trimmed to the exact measurements dictated in the BOM's instructions. And, after several months, Alice won the drawing. She seemed pleased, taking home twenty-five blocks made by various guild members.

A couple of weeks later, she shared a secret with a handful of friends who met in her house for a bee.

"I got those blocks home and measured them. Would you believe they were all different sizes? Some were twelve inches, some were eleven and one-half inches, and some were as large as twelve and one-half inches! And," her voice lowered to a whisper, "a lot of them weren't pieced well. Some seams didn't meet, and some points weren't very pointy!"

She straightened her shoulders and declared, "Of course I knew what I had to do. I took them all apart and pieced those blocks again–every one of them. It was a lot of work, but now I have a perfect quilt top, one I can be proud of!"

The following month, Rita won the block-of-the-month drawing. Like Alice, she took her blocks home and measured them, finding them to be less than uniform. She also found a few blocks that were poorly pieced.

But unlike Alice, she didn't take them apart. She wanted to preserve the work of her sister quilters, even if it wasn't perfect. So, before piecing the blocks together, she designed a new method of sashing, to allow for the various sized blocks. Some sashing was wide; some was narrow. The completed quilt top had a modern, artsy look to it. While not all points were pointy and not all seams matched properly, the overall look was rich and interesting.

Both Alice and Rita entered their finished quilts in area shows and fairs. Each won awards. Which was the better piecing method? Neither. Each woman simply approached her problem with a solution that was right for her. Alice wanted perfection; Rita wanted personality, and they each achieved the desired goal.

The Quilting Frame: It's wonderful to have the patience, like Alice, simply to start over when we make mistakes. But it's also wonderful to be forgiven and accepted just the way we are. Jesus loves perfection because it demonstrates the beauty of God, yet He loves people who are not perfect. Our imperfections shame us from approaching our Heavenly Father, so Jesus, who is perfect, offers to make up the difference we each need to become perfect in the eyes of God. Some of us are a half-inch short of fitting God's template, while others of us are so over-zealous we still miss the square. But, like Rita's sashing, Jesus evens out the differences so that we can all receive the high prize of knowing God intimately.

God's Template: "For the wages which sin pays is death, but the [bountiful] free gift of God is eternal life through (in union with) Jesus Christ our Lord" (Romans 6:23 AMPLIFIED).

The Binding Stitch: Lord, I love what is right, but I don't have power always to carry it out. Thank You for accepting me the way I am and binding me into Your family quilt.

Scrap Bag: Before you cut pieces for an entire quilt, cut enough for only one sample block. This will allow you to try the block, checking for pattern accuracy, color coordination, and ease of construction. If you make the block and don't like it, you haven't wasted much time or fabric.

The Quilt Gift

My mother's hands, gnarled with arthritis, worked at the quilt frame each evening. She loved quilting, and I as a teenager loved watching her. This effort would be her final masterpiece. It was beautiful in its simplicity: pink roses with green leaves appliquéd onto a muslin background. The eight-inch blocks alternated with plain muslin squares, which were quilted in the same rose-shaped design as the appliqué.

Through the winter she quilted, and by spring she was finished. She carefully folded the quilt and placed it in the linen closet. Every few months, she'd take this and other stored quilts and lay them on the bed, recall the memories, and refold them. This refolding, she explained, was important so the quilt wouldn't acquire permanent creases. One time she'd fold vertically; the next time horizontally.

Sometimes she'd fold inside out; other times, outside in. The quilts were never stored in plastic, she said, because that could cause mildew. She cared about her quilts and took measures to preserve them.

After the deaths of our parents, we five siblings began the difficult process of dividing their belongings. We gave the rose quilt to Bob, because he was the oldest. I recited to him the litany of folding instructions I'd remembered from Mother. Then, we packed it with other things for Bob and his wife, Pat.

Much to my surprise, at a family reunion a few years later they gave the quilt back to me. "We want you to have it, since you were with Mother when she made it," they explained. "We know you'll take good care of it." I was pleased and grateful, almost awestruck, that the quilt should be mine. Each year I used it as a bedcover for a month or so, enjoying the beautiful roses and remembering the hands that lovingly fashioned them.

When Bob and Pat's first grandson was to marry, I wanted to give him a special gift—one reflecting family and love. The rose quilt came to mind, but I quickly discarded the idea. It was mine. How could I let it go? Yet, no gift I could buy would hold such personal and heartfelt meaning for Neil and Tonya. I spread it on the bed one last time and took a couple of snapshots. Then I wrote the instructions for care, along with a history of the quilt and of the hands which stitched it.

Wrapping Mother's rose quilt, packing it in a box, taking it to the shipping outlet, all strained my emotions. What if they didn't like it?

After all, Neil only vaguely remembered his great-grandmother, and Tonya hadn't known her at all. What if they didn't understand the quilt's sentimental value? What if they wouldn't care for it reverently? Pushing aside my reservations, I paid the shipping costs and walked away.

A week later, a thank-you note declared my fears to be unfounded. The young couple were thrilled with the quilt, affirming my decision to give it and assuring me they would follow Mother's instructions for care. Someday, they said, they'd pass the quilt to another generation.

The Quilting Frame: I hadn't really owned that quilt; I was only a steward of it. The same is now true of Neil and Tonya. Likewise, followers of Jesus in the New Testament Book of Acts held their possessions loosely, often giving them away to benefit someone else. (The story of their benevolence is found in Acts 2:42–47.) Clinging too tightly to something can rob us of the joy of giving and can rob others of the joy of receiving.

God's Template: "Give generously to him and do so without a grudging heart; then because of this the LORD your God will bless you in all your work and in everything you put your hand to" (Deuteronomy 15:10).

The Binding Stitch: Loose me, Lord, from the fear of giving, adorn me with a generous heart, and anoint the work of my hands to bless the generations that will come after me.

Scrap Bag: Always store quilts carefully. Some quilt shops have acid-free paper, which can be used to wrap your quilts or to line the shelves on which you store them. Refold quilts every three months.

Nelanna's Quilt

Nelanna Lillehagen of Queensland is only six years old, but her name is well known among quilters throughout Australia.

At age three, she was diagnosed with acute lymphoblastic leukemia, a high-risk condition because of its effects on the cerebral spinal fluid. Such a case is rare for a child so young. Doctors prescribed chemotherapy and radiation, and now she is in remission. If, however, Nelanna comes out of remission, there is no further treatment currently available. But research continues, and new developments may be just over the horizon. She goes to the children's hospital in Brisbane every three months for checkups.

Nelanna's family enjoyed the hospitality of the Ronald McDonald house during one of her hospital visits. Before returning home, the child asked to see the room where her family had stayed.

She noticed a quilt on her sister's Ronald McDonald bed, and she told her mother she wished she could have one like it someday. Later, Catherine Lillehagen casually mentioned the incident to her friend Hilary Joy Laughton, not realizing that Hilary was a quilter.

Catherine soon forgot the conversation, but Hilary didn't. She talked with a few friends in her Internet quilting group, the Southern Cross On-line Quilters of Australia and New Zealand. They decided on nine-inch blocks and began spreading the word. Within six weeks they received enough patchwork for a quilt top.

But, Hilary says, "The blocks just kept coming in. Day after day there would be more in my letterbox. People were getting their friends to make them. People were sending in one, two, sometimes four blocks!" Altogether, she received seventy-two, including two from the United States.

Hilary began setting them together with the help of her local quilting group, the Arts & Craft Patchworkers of Tenterfield, New South Wales. They realized some blocks were larger and some were smaller than the nine inches originally requested. With these they designed a pieced backing for the quilt, in addition to the quilt top. The backing would include odd-size blocks as well as a beautiful rainbow panel which someone contributed. Hilary pieced the top and the back, then machine-quilted the layers together, finishing in time for Nelanna's homecoming after her last chemo treatment.

Hilary remembers the child's reaction to the bright quilt.

"Nelanna was totally amazed as were her sister and mother, who were both present when the quilt was handed over," she says. "I guess we all had tears in our eyes for a few minutes. Her joy at seeing the quilt made it all worthwhile. Nelanna's mother Catherine was thrilled to think that so many people whom she didn't know made this special quilt for her little girl."

The Quilting Frame: God enjoys giving us the little things that we desire, in hopes that it will build our faith to ask for bigger things. Nothing is too hard for God. From the four corners of the earth, He can hold back the winds (Revelation 7:1) or call forth His people (Isaiah 11:12) to make a quilt for a little girl in Australia. Jesus said, "Therefore I say unto you, What things soever ye desire, when ye pray, believe that ye receive them, and ye shall have them" (Mark 11:24 KJV).

God's Template: LORD, You have heard the desire of the humble; You will prepare their heart; You will cause Your ear to hear" (Psalm 10:17 NKJV).

The Binding Stitch: I delight in You, Lord, and You give me the desires and secret petitions of my heart (Psalm 37:4 AMPLIFIED).

Scrap Bag: A new product on the market allows you to put fabric into your computer printer. You buy muslin in eight-and-one-half-by-eleven-inch pieces, prepared with a stiff backing. You can use these to transfer photographs or other images from your computer. You may also use them to record the history of your quilts. Select a large font, so the words can be easily read, and write the date(s) of piecing and quilting, the name(s) of piecer and quilter, and any other special information. After printing, peel off the stiff backing and sew the muslin onto the back of the quilt.

Family Reunion Quilt

Hi, I'm Bob and Kate's daughter Ruth. How are you related to me?"

With that line, I became acquainted with dozens of cousins. I also used it as a springboard for a major quilt project.

The idea started years earlier, at the annual McHaney reunion in Leachville, Arkansas. I'd attended regularly since childhood, but the family was growing faster than I could keep up. Marriages, in-laws, births, adoptions, foster children—it was more than my mind could handle, especially since I didn't see most of them the rest of the year. And I noticed that some of us at the reunion chatted with our closer kin rather than approaching a third cousin once-removed, whose name we didn't know anyway. With nearly one hundred people converging on the front lawn of that farmhouse, a person could easily miss a few relatives.

What was worse, some of the older folks were beginning to pass from the scene. Grandpa and Grandma McHaney were already gone, as was one precious uncle.

It was time to act. Months before the next reunion, I planned a family album quilt. It wouldn't be full of fancy piecework or gaudy colors, because the signatures should stand out. It would be big— big enough to accommodate scores of names. So, I decided on a queen-size quilt with a simple pinwheel pattern, each block surrounded by rectangular signature blocks. I chose small prints on dark backgrounds for the pinwheels, and unbleached muslin for the signatures.

After planning and cutting, I gathered a hundred of the muslin pieces and my sketch of the pattern, and headed for the reunion.

I had a wonderful time meeting people, and we all enjoyed answering the question, "How are you related to me?" We laughed and joked and recalled fond memories. Most precious to me were the moments I spent with the older aunts and uncles, who relished the idea of a family quilt.

Since a few relatives couldn't attend the reunion that year, I decided not to finish the quilt right away. The next summer, and the next, I patiently returned for more signatures, until I had 130 total. I spent some of my free time each winter embroidering the names and piecing the pinwheels, then did the final layout and quilting when all the signatures were collected.

Four years after the first muslin block was signed, I brought a finished quilt. Aunt Nan strung a clothesline in the front yard, and we hung it for all to see. The local newspaper even sent a photographer to capture and publicize the moment.

I still have the quilt, and someday I'll pass it down to a grandchild or great-grandchild, whose name isn't even on it. In the meantime, I use it occasionally on the bed, and I enjoy remembering the family it represents.

To me, the McHaney Reunion quilt is more than a record of an extended family; it's the tool I used to reconnect me to my heritage.

The Quilting Frame: Cornelius was a man who wanted to be a part of God's family, but he was not Jewish. The story in Acts 10 gives a fascinating account of how Peter, who previously had explained only to Jews about salvation through Jesus Christ, was convinced by God to speak to Cornelius. God gave Peter a vision of a large sheet lowered from heaven, on which were all kinds of animals forbidden by his Jewish faith to eat; yet God told Peter to partake of them. Through this unusual visual aid, Peter came to understand that

God welcomes everyone into His family.

God's Template: " Then Peter began to speak: 'I now realize how true it is that God does not show favoritism but accepts men from every nation who fear him and do what is right' " (Acts 10:34–35).

The Binding Stitch: Thank You for including me in all of the promises You have made to Your children.

Scrap Bag: Avoid direct sunlight on quilts. Even an hour of sunshine can fade cotton fabric. Whether quilts are stored on shelves, hanging on walls, or covering beds, keep window shades drawn during the time the sun might shine on them.

The Sick Quilt

When cold and flu season strikes, I reach for the Sick Quilt.

The quilt isn't sick, of course, but I use it when *I'm* sick. It's too short for a bed, but it's perfect to snuggle under while I'm recuperating on the sofa, sniffling and coughing and sipping hot tea. It's an ideal companion when I must nurse myself back to health and only feel strong enough to peruse quilt magazines.

The Sick Quilt came from special friends at a quilt guild in Texas where I served a term as president. The guild traditionally gave each outgoing president a quilt made by the membership. The construction of this quilt was coordinated by the previous president, and the finished product was presented to the retiring leader as she left office.

Overseeing this quilting project was quite a job. The former president had to figure out the colors and patterns most likely to please her successor, purchase fabrics and other materials, enlist members to prepare and distribute fabric packets and patterns to each participant, keep up with the returned quilt blocks, piece the quilt top, then schedule quilting bees for it. All the while, she must try to keep the work a secret from the current president and finish it in time for the appropriate guild meeting. Occasionally this involved some last-minute, late-night bees, but the quilt was always finished on schedule, much to the delight of the recipient.

The year I was president was a little different. I didn't realize until later that my predecessor, a busy young mother, simply couldn't find time to properly organize the president's quilt project because of family obligations.

Nonetheless, she did the best she could. Knowing I loved triangles, she called all members just a few days before the deadline. She asked them to make a twelve-and-one-half-inch block from their own fabric stash, using a technique known as Perfectly Pieced Triangles, which we'd learned at a guild workshop earlier that year. They brought their blocks to the meeting, and behind my back she stacked them neatly in a quilt-motif sack. At the appropriate moment, she presented the sack to me.

I knew immediately, upon accepting the sack, that it didn't contain a finished quilt. I also knew that my predecessor had had some pressing family situations in the past few months. And, I could see the unmistakable look of remorse and apology on her face when she made the presentation.

I accepted the blocks gracefully, hugging her and thanking her for them. I held each one up for the group to see, and promised to piece the quilt within the month. Soon the members were organizing bees to help me with the quilting. It wasn't long before the quilt was finished and displayed at a guild meeting.

Now, when I look at the Sick Quilt, I think of my friend, who fulfilled an obligation in the midst of many other commitments. I also think of the guild members whose names grace the blocks, and of the members whose quilting stitches hold them together. And when I'm sick, I'm thankful for them all and for the comfort the quilt brings to me.

The Quilting Frame: Teamwork is a vital part of quilting, as is the support we give to each other in the building of our faith. Scriptures tell us to pray for one another that we might ourselves be healed. Everyone shares the happiness when our collective petitions are answered.

God's Template: "We have set our hope that he [Jesus] will continue to deliver us, as you help us by your prayers. Then many will give thanks on our behalf for the gracious favor granted us in answer to the prayers of many" (2 Corinthians 1:10–11).

The Binding Stitch: Lord, cause my love for others to increase with each stitch I make.

Scrap Bag: In many quilt shops, you'll find "quilters' quarters." These are quarter-yard lengths of fabrics already cut and priced, especially for quilters who want to add to their stash. Sometimes you'll find "fat quarters," a more generous cut for the same price as regular quarters.

What's in a Name?

Do you always call your husband 'Mark Danner'?" The question arises during conversations with new friends.

"Nearly always," I explain. And then they have to ask, "But why? Most people call their spouses by first names only."

I proceed to tell them:

Three or four years after our marriage, my husband and I traveled from our home in South Carolina to visit my parents at their cottage in Michigan's Upper Peninsula. The drive was long, and neither of us felt well. I'd had some unexplained digestive problems, and Mark had endured a fierce headache driving in a heavy rainstorm the last few hours of the trip.

When we arrived—about 11 P.M.—Mother greeted us at the door and ushered us into a house full of nieces and nephews whom

Mark had never met. Happy to see everyone, we visited for a while but asked to be excused as the weariness of the trip and our fragile health began to wear on us. Mother, always the hostess, bustled around, settling everyone in spare beds, recliners, sofas, and pallets on the floor. She put me and Mark in the front bedroom and hauled out a stack of quilts from the closet.

"Remember this one?" She pointed to a quilt made by her mother years earlier. "The Churn Dash pattern was one of your grandma's favorites, though I never liked that yellow background." Next she unfolded a blue and white star quilt. "Of course the colors are much better here—not so scrappy." We realized that Mother would not let us rest until we'd seen the whole collection. Quilt after quilt was spread out, each with its own story. Mark and I listened politely until finally one was chosen for the bed and the others laid aside.

Mother left the room, and I closed the door behind her. Mark immediately fell into bed and pulled the Churn Dash quilt around him. I took off my shoes and rummaged through a suitcase for pajamas. Just as I crawled into the bed, Mother opened the door again.

"Everybody OK in here? Need any more quilts?" Her voice was loud, considering the time of night and our tiredness.

"Yes, Mother," I whispered, trying to establish a quieter tone of voice. "Mark's already asleep."

"MIKE? Mike who?" Mother's tone was urgent, almost panicky.

Perhaps in the confusion of all the overnight company, she'd put me in with the wrong relative.

"No, not Mike," I assured her. "Mark—Mark Danner."

"Oh, well," her voice was still loud, but relieved. She increased the volume a bit more, to be heard across the room. "Goodnight, MARK DANNER!"

Everyone in the house overheard the exchange, and from that moment, the family called him Mark Danner, saying the name as if it were one word. And so do I.

The Quilting Frame: Misunderstandings over names can be comical. It's unfortunate, however, that many people do not know that the name "Jesus" means, "God with us." And within the meaning of God's name is every provision that we crave both inside and outside of trouble. In fact, the Bible provides hundreds of metaphors and explanations to help us understand God's *full* name. Some references to His name reveal Him as healer, strength, refuge, shield, fountain, shade, creator, judge, song, and rock, as well as father, king, redeemer, and shepherd. He poured all of

Himself into Jesus (Colossians 2:9), so we could say His name as if it were one word.

God's Template: Jesus said, "I will do [I Myself will grant] whatever you ask in My Name [as presenting all that I AM], so that the Father may be glorified and extolled in (through) the Son" (John 14:14 AMPLIFIED).

The Binding Stitch: Thank You, Jesus, for being all that we need.

Scrap Bag: Do you enjoy looking at quilt books but don't want to invest a small fortune in them? Consider a second-hand bookstore or a library. Also, your quilt guild may have a library of sorts. If they don't, why not help start one?

$\mathcal{Q}$uilting $\mathcal{C}$orrespondence

Some people say the international language is Morse code; others say it's music.

But I vote for quilting.

At my husband's workplace, he meets many Japanese people. One became a good friend, and when her family made a trip to the U.S., we invited them into our home for a meal. We were a little nervous about the dinner party. After all, mother and father only spoke a smattering of English, not enough for an extended conversation. We knew we'd have to rely on the daughter to translate for us.

The meal went fairly well, punctuated occasionally with small talk about foods and the weather. We smiled and gestured often, but I wished we could have talked more, because the conversation lulled at times. After eating, my husband showed the father his computer.

And I invited mother and daughter to my sewing room.

I showed my works in progress, my stash of fabrics, my stack of finished quilts. I showed my current quilt on the frame and sat for a moment to demonstrate my quilting technique. I showed pictures of quilts I'd made and sold, as well as my plans for future quilts. I showed my library of quilting books and patterns.

The two Japanese women came alive! They exclaimed over different things in the room and spoke together in soft voices, with the daughter sometimes translating a question or comment for me.

After examining everything, the mother shyly spoke: "May I use sewing machine, please?"

I grabbed a piece of fabric and turned on the machine. Within seconds she was stitching, getting a feel for the speed, trying various settings. I pressed a few buttons and let her sew her name on the cloth. She stitched it twice, quickly, before stopping.

Her newfound enthusiasm was transforming. Since entering the sewing room, she somehow felt more comfortable using her limited English skills, and she told me she liked to sew. In fact, she said, her friend in Japan was a professional quilter.

When the family left our house that afternoon, they took with them a few souvenirs from us: candy from a local company, some small quilted wall hangings I'd made, and a scrap of calico with a sampling of stitches. In turn, they gave us beautiful Japanese souvenirs, including a rich-textured indigo fabric and a bright red silk.

But the best gift was the friendship I established with the mother. In the few years since that meeting, we've corresponded by mail, with a little help for me from local Japanese friends. Maybe I'm not good at speaking Japanese, but I do speak quilting, which I've discovered is an effective international language.

The Quilting Frame: God's language is difficult to understand, too. He uses complex terms, such as love, forgiveness, grace, and mercy. That is why Jesus used visual aids to communicate the point He was making. "Look at the lilies," He once said. "Consider how they neither toil nor spin, yet Solomon in all his magnificence was not arrayed like them. If God so clothes the grass of the field, will He not much more surely clothe you?" (Matthew 6:25–34, author's paraphrase).

God's Template: "In the same way, the Spirit helps us in our weakness. We do not know what we ought to pray for, but the Spirit himself intercedes for us with groans that words cannot express" (Romans 8:26).

The Binding Stitch: Your love for me is too great to understand, but thank You for Your unrelenting effort to explain it to me.

Scrap Bag: What's the advantage of hand-quilting over machine-quilting? To an untrained eye, they look the same. However, if you want an authentic, traditional quilt, you'll probably want it hand-quilted. A fast quilter can hand-quilt a bedcover in four to eight weeks, depending on the quilting design and the size of the quilt. But, if you want a durable quilt that will hold up under lots of wear and washings, you might want it machine-quilted. You can machine-quilt at your own machine, with or without a frame. But, you may struggle a bit with a large quilt. You may prefer to have it machine-quilted by a professional, who can do the job in a few hours.

Saying Thanks

A quilter in Michigan knows the value of saying thanks.

Ellen Ann Bidigare is the regional chairperson for Tiny Miracles, a group that makes and donates up to one hundred baby quilts each month to local hospitals for use in their neonatal units. Premature babies and others with health difficulties receive the Tiny Miracles quilts. Such colorful bedcovers are often a bright spot in an otherwise difficult time in the families' lives.

"Seldom," Ellen says, "do I get parents who actually call our office, or drop a note of thanks, but I understand. They're so busy, enduring the stress of having their infant in the hospital day in and day out." Nevertheless, she knows the quilts are appreciated, so she and the others continue to make them.

One day at Tiny Miracles, the phone rang. "A dad wanted to

thank me for all the beautiful quilts our local hospital had received," Ellen recalls. He was especially thankful for the little quilt his son got while in the neonatal intensive care unit. He explained to Ellen that his pregnant wife had died as the result of a car accident. Their baby was delivered by C-section in the emergency room.

This dad was now at home alone, taking care of the newborn son. Ellen says, "He took the time to call and let me know we are doing a great job here, donating quilts for the babies. He said the quilt meant so much, almost like a gentle touch from an angel."

Ellen uses this illustration to point out that serving others is important and is appreciated. "Our quilting talent should be shared, whether by teaching or by donating a finished quilt here and there. Please keep your heart open when you can. It really does make a difference!"

The Quilting Frame: Quilts are synonymous with comfort, and comfort is an antidote for hardships. The Good News that Jesus proclaimed did not promise we would avoid hardships, but He did promise to be a comfort in times of trouble. The apostle Paul suffered many hardships but still encouraged people to remain true to the faith. In 2 Corinthians 1:8–9, he admitted, "We were under great pressure, far beyond our ability to endure, so that we despaired even of life. Indeed, in our hearts we felt the sentence of death. But this happened that we might not rely on ourselves but on God, who raises the dead." As a quilt covers our coldness, God's promise of redemption covers our loss.

God's Template: Jesus said, "The Spirit of the Lord is upon me, because he hath anointed me to preach the gospel to the poor; he hath sent me to heal the brokenhearted, to preach deliverance to the captives, and recovering of sight to the blind, to set at liberty them that are bruised" (Luke 4:18 KJV).

The Binding Stitch: I praise You, Father of our Lord Jesus Christ, the Father of compassion and the God of all comfort, who comforts us in all our troubles, so that we can comfort those in any trouble with the comfort we ourselves have received from God (2 Corinthians 1:3–4).

Scrap Bag: When you're in a store that sells fabric, check out the remnants bin. You may find a quarter-yard of a cotton print which you'll need for an upcoming project. Quilters are known for their "stashes" of fabric. You can collect a little at a time to make your stash grow.

Miz' Pearl

Newly married in the 1940s, Barbara Francis learned the importance of connections.

She found herself in Sassafrass, Kentucky, visiting her new in-laws for the first time. The streets were dirt; the houses were cabins and tar-paper shacks; and the people were poor farmers, scraping out a living in post-depression America.

Even so, her husband's family welcomed her joyfully, and she visited in many homes, getting to know cousins, aunts, uncles, grandparents, and others. Early in her stay in Sassafrass, Barbara sat on a front porch with Cousin Inez. As they talked, they noticed a neighbor settling herself into a rocking chair on a porch across the road.

"Hey, Miz' Pearl!" Inez's voice rose above the drone of honeybees and flies. "Mind if we step over for a spell?"

Without a word, the elderly Pearl gestured affirmatively, and Inez led young Barbara across the dusty road. Inez cheerfully introduced Barbara to the older woman, but Miss Pearl hardly gave her a second glance. Instead, she offered Inez the only other chair on the porch, forcing Barbara to stand nearby.

Inez tried the introduction again. This time Barbara extended her hand to Miss Pearl, but the reaction was almost the same. "Hmmm," Pearl intoned before turning back to Inez. "She's just a young 'un."

"Yes," agreed Inez. "She is young, but she's newly married, and we was wonderin' if you could spare one or two of your quilts to git her started off right."

Miss Pearl's lips creased into one thin line. "Ain't got none."

"What? I saw a whole stack of 'em over here jist a few weeks ago! What happened to 'em?"

"They's all gone now." Pearl crossed her arms as if to conclude the conversation, and Inez realized she needed another approach.

"Miz' Pearl," she began sweetly, "you remember little Martin Francis? Used to play in your yard. Grew up and went away to school."

"Yep, I 'member. Sweet kid. Sometimes brought me blackberries from his pickin'. His daddy's one of the best men in the county. His granny and I was friends till she passed on. I jist love that family." She paused to scratch a couple of chigger bites on her ankle.

"Why's you ask?"

Inez gestured to Barbara. "This here girl is Martin's new wife!"

Miss Pearl's face changed in a moment, from distant and un-friendly to gracious and warm. "Well, well, why didn't ye jist say so?" She left her rocker and took Barbara's hand, leading her into the tiny house. On the bed were dozens of beautiful handmade quilts, spread flat. After showing each of them to Barbara, she invited the young bride to choose two to keep, refusing even the mention of money.

Barbara was overwhelmed by Miss Pearl's sudden generosity. She realized the change in the woman's attitude had nothing to do with Barbara herself. Rather, it was because of her relationship with someone else in the community. It pays to have connections with important people, even in Sassafrass, Kentucky.

Quilting Frame: Just as Miss Pearl saved her best gifts for her own "adopted" family, God gives His best gifts to those who say, "Jesus is my Lord." To His own family, God gives spiritual insights that will illuminate our lives for good. To some He gives the power to speak wisdom to a person who doesn't know what to do, and to another He gives a word of understanding that brings peace in the midst of chaos (1 Corinthians 12). But just as Barbara had not *done* anything to deserve one of Miss Pearl's quilts, we cannot deserve God's gifts. His grace is offered to us because of who we are in Christ, not because of what we have done.

God's Template: "I will take you as my own people, and I will be your God. Then you will know that I am the LORD your God, who brought you out from under the yoke of the Egyptians [slavery]" (Exodus 6:7, [author's paraphrase]).

The Binding Stitch: Thank You for claiming me as Your own and for giving to me undeserved covering for otherwise cold nights.

Scrap Bag: Resist the temptation to include old fabric with new in a quilt which will receive considerable use. The old cloth will not hold together well, and the quilt will often need repairs.

The Hug Quilt

Dale Ann Potter knows what a hug feels like: It feels like a quilt.

Following cancer surgery and six weeks of chemotherapy and radiation treatments, she was "down in the dumps and not too cheery." Most cancer survivors can empathize. They know the weeks, months, even years, of trying to get life back to normal. Friends can't always understand what they're going through. They experience levels of discouragement and depression which others cannot fathom.

But they also know that one friendly gesture can make the difference in their outlook and in their determination to recuperate. In Dale's case, a friend from her quilting group, the Black Gold Quilt Patch in Leduc, Alberta, Canada, stopped by. After several minutes of cheerful conversation, she reached into her bag and produced a twin-size quilt.

"We got together and made you a Hug Quilt," she explained to Dale. Indeed, fourteen friendship blocks made by fourteen friends were united with blue sashings. A horse, a frog, and a Sunbonnet Sue marched among other colorful blocks. On the border words such as "joy," "hopeful," "love," "hugs," and "Our Friend Always, Dale Potter" were stitched. The quilt was machine-quilted, ready for Dale's snuggling.

And snuggle she did. Overwhelmed by their thoughtfulness, she says, "I was in tears for days. Whenever I felt like needing a hug, I wrapped myself in that quilt."

Today, the quilt hangs in the loft of her shop, the Red Barn Quilting & Tea Room in Oyen, Alberta, where she lives and teaches quilting classes. Because of its easy visibility, she sees the quilt often. "Every time I look at it, it gives me strength and a hug."

The Quilting Frame: Sometimes words are not enough. A hug is an active expression that says, "I embrace you, I want you to *feel* my love and concern for you as I hold you close to me." God said that faith without works, or corresponding actions, is dead. Love is a verb. If we say we love someone, our deeds should demonstrate grace and mercy.

God's Template: "A man will be satisfied with good by the fruit of his words, and the deeds of a man's hands will return to him" (Proverbs 12:14 NASB).

The Binding Stitch: Although we can't see You, Lord, we can feel Your presence when we love one another (1 John 4:12).

Scrap Bag: Most quilters prefer using 100 percent cotton fabrics, rather than blends, when piecing their quilts. Every piece of cotton fabric behaves in about the same way, so you'll have no surprises if you stay with only cotton. But if you use polyester or other fabrics along with cotton, your finished quilt may shrink in unexpected places during washing.

Grandmother's Thimble

I knew this was a quilter's house the moment I stepped through the front door. Beth's living room contained none of the normal furniture—no sofa, no coffee table, no end tables with lamps, no family portrait over the mantel. Instead, I saw a sewing machine, serger, quilt frame, bolts of fabric, and a wall full of projects-in-progress.

"This isn't the formal living room," she explained as she guided me around a layout of quilt blocks on the floor. "But it's where I do most of *my* living! The rest of the family can have the den." As a sister quilter, I understood. Here were her favorite things, all in one room, all within easy access. While it's a little unconventional to convert the front room into a sewing center, it worked for her and her family.

I admired her projects, exclaimed over her new machines, and complimented her stash of beautiful fabrics. But what really caught my eye was her thimble collection.

She had several shadow boxes and display cases filled with them: thimbles picturing famous landmarks, thimbles marking special events, thimbles commemorating holidays and anniversaries; thimbles for impossibly large fingers, thimbles for children's fingers. Some were antiques, while others were new. Many were strictly for decoration, but some were serviceable.

"How many of these things do you have?" I couldn't contain my amazement.

"Oh, a couple hundred, maybe more," she shrugged. "I stopped counting long ago."

After my visit to Beth's, I decided to begin my own thimble collection.

I had a couple of old thimbles—the worn-out kind with holes. I had a couple of plastic souvenir thimbles and a stiff leather thimble which I didn't often use. My collection had meager beginnings, but after telling others about the new hobby, I soon acquired more thimbles.

Two had tiny drawings of pianos, given by my music students.

Another sported a bright red Arkansas Razorback, from my family's home state.

A third was a pewter miniature of the Space Needle in Seattle, from my husband's business trip.

The most precious thimble has a different story, though. My mother-in-law, while spring housecleaning, came across something she'd inherited from *her* mother-in-law some years earlier: a tiny thimble, hardly big enough to fit her pinky finger.

As she turned it over in her palm, she recalled the story of a young man, John Danner, giving his bride a special gift on their wedding day. It was a gift she would treasure and use as a quilter throughout their fifty-four-year marriage. It would always remind her of him; each time she wore it she would see their wedding date engraved on it: 11-25-16.

This ten-karat gold thimble now rests safely in my shadow box. When I see it I think of the diminutive woman who was my grandmother-in-law for only a brief time before her death. My collection of thimbles may never reach the extent of Beth's, but this tiny addition is much more valuable to me.

The Quilting Frame: Like the thimble-covered finger, some
of the most outstanding work in the home, the church,
and the community is done by those who are never
seen by the crowds. It is good to give thanks for the

strength of the small, humble parts of the body. Grandfather Danner was wise to honor the value in Grandmother's tiny finger.

God's Template: "The head cannot say to the feet, 'I don't need you!' On the contrary, those parts of the body that seem to be weaker are indispensable" (1 Corinthians 12:21–22).

The Binding Stitch: Bless my hands, Lord, to be ready to serve others, no matter how large or how small the task.

Scrap Bag: Use specified quilting thread when hand-quilting. It's stronger than regular thread and will hold your quilt secure for many years. However, don't try this standard, cotton quilting thread in your sewing machine. Most machines don't handle it well. If you're doing machine-quilting, ask for recommendations from the quilt or craft store. They may show you a clear thread, which looks and feels like thin fishing line. This is popular among many machine-quilters.

A Special Class

Seven pairs of eyes stared at me with a mixture of curiosity, friendship, and hope, and I knew in that moment I'd have to change my perception of "special education."

Since my early days in college, I'd aspired to be a teacher. I envisioned myself before an enthusiastic group of high school English students eager to memorize vocabulary words, tackle Shakespeare, and write research papers. Instead, circumstances led me to teach kindergarten and, later, sixth grade.

But I avoided special education. In college I thought, *Only martyrs major in special ed. Why would they elect to work with students who had mental, emotional, or physical handicaps? Isn't a "normal" class enough of a challenge?*

That's why I balked when my friend Michelle, a special education teacher in a public school, invited me to present a quilting demonstration to her class. Her students, she explained, were middle-schoolers with a variety of problems, rendering them unable to function in mainstream classrooms. I imagined a mob of wild kids who screamed, kicked, and ran uncontrollably about the room.

A hundred excuses came to mind, but nothing seemed sincere. Reluctantly I packed my supplies and drove to the school. There I met Michelle and her seven students.

They all sat at their tables.

They wiggled but watched my every move.

They asked questions and told quilt stories of their own.

They tried a few stitches on the demonstrator blocks I'd brought.

They fingered my small quilt in the hoop and applauded my large quilts on display.

They were fun!

And "special education" took on a new meaning for me that day. I'm now more compassionate toward the variety of people who cross my path, thanks to Michelle's class and my quilts.

The Quilting Frame: God made each of us differently—as
varied as the colors, shapes, and patterns of the quilts

I make. Not just the "red, brown, yellow, black, and white" kind of diversity we sing about in Sunday school; this variance goes deeper. The Old Testament psalmist wrote, "I am fearfully and wonderfully made." He knew the uniqueness of each individual– mentally, physically, emotionally, spiritually. He viewed each person as precious in God's sight.

God's Template: "Then Peter began to speak: 'I now realize how true it is that God does not show favoritism but accepts men from every nation who fear him and do what is right' " (Acts 10:34–35).

The Binding Stitch: Lord, open my ears to hear the special education of Your wisdom.

Scrap Bag: When demonstrating quilting to children, I prepare a simple four-patch block for each child. I cut backing and batting to fit, and I thread plenty of needles. At the demonstration, I let each child layer his or her own "quilt" and make some quilting stitches, then keep the block.

E-Support

It's been three years since I received this wonderful gift, but even now as I write, the tears come."

Linda Kau's statement reflects the emotion she still feels when remembering how a stack of quilt blocks helped her through a difficult situation.

Her mother was diagnosed with a malignant brain tumor and given only a few months to live. "Needless to say, I was devastated. Mom was my best friend," she says. But Linda did have other friends—quilting friends she met on the Internet. She turned to them with her problem.

"They'd already cheered with me through the birth of my first grandchild. Now I asked for cheer of another kind." In response, messages of support were immediately posted for Linda from across the country and across the world. But that wasn't the end of it.

One day a local friend from this E-mail group called and invited her to lunch. The friend said she was moving and wanted to get together one last time. They met on a warm summer afternoon, sitting at the café's outdoor table. Linda remembers, "As we neared the end of our lunch she pulled out a gift box. She said that our on-line group wanted to send something to help me through these tough times ahead."

By now, Linda's emotions gave way and tears began to flow. "I opened the box and found dozens of beautiful heart blocks, with sentiments and names written on them. I took the box back to work with me and showed them to my co-workers. Then I went home to share them with Mom—one of the last special things we did together."

Today, Linda is still amazed at the quilters' display of love and support. She points out that all but four of those heart blocks were made by people she'd never met in person.

She hasn't yet decided what to do with the blocks. Should she piece them into a quilt? What piecing layout should she use? She has a few ideas, but nothing seems quite right. Even so, they're valuable as they are. "Perhaps one reason I haven't put them together," Linda says, "is that they remind me of the day Mom and I sat and enjoyed the gift. Perhaps this is the way they should remain—a reminder of that special day."

The Quilting Frame: Many small contributions or expressions of love can have a life-changing impact on someone else. Too often, we procrastinate a small act of kindness, thinking we should wait until we can make a larger display of our attention. But God can take an insignificant thing given in love, and multiply that expression in an overwhelming experience of grace and mercy.

God's Template: "But now for a brief moment grace has been shown from the LORD our God, to leave us an escaped remnant and to give us a peg in His holy place, that our God may enlighten our eyes and grant us a little reviving in our bondage" (Ezra 9:8 NASB).

The Binding Stitch: The more I know You, Lord, the more grace [undeserved favor] and peace [which is perfect well-being, all necessary good, all spiritual prosperity, and freedom from fears] abound in my life (2 Peter 1:2 AMPLIFIED).

Scrap Bag: Are you a web surfer? You can learn a lot from quilters on the Internet. Many quilt magazines, quilt guilds and quilt teachers have websites with free patterns, on-line lessons, opportunities for charity work, and chat rooms to answer your quilting questions. Try this site as a starting place: www.quiltmag.com.

The Christmas Card Quilt

Christmas often brings surprises, but when Linda in Minnesota received a Christmas card from Michigan with a likeness of her own quilt on it, she could hardly believe it.

The incident began more than a year earlier. Making a baby quilt for a family friend who was about to become a grandfather, Linda selected mauve and pale green fabrics, pieced the quilt, then hand-quilted it. Pleased with the result, she sent it to the family in Michigan and resumed her own projects.

Later, the couple called to tell Linda how they liked the quilt. They jokingly bantered with her about the quilt's true owners. Grandpa had delivered it to the parents-to-be, but Grandma wanted it back with her, to use when the baby came to visit. After getting many thanks from the grandparents, Linda hung up the phone, happy that her quilt had been appreciated. But surprising news came a short time later. The grandparents called again to say there would be twins, not just one!

Linda rushed back to the fabric store. She found more mauve and green for another quilt to complement the first. One night during the quiltmaking process, she couldn't sleep, so she decided to stitch a quick Irish Chain quilt for the twins' grandmother, using red and dark green fabric that she had in her stash. After a couple of weeks of hand-quilting, she shipped the two quilts to Michigan, making sure the recipients knew the red and green one was for Grandma.

"Everyone was very happy with the quilts," Linda remembers. "I got lots of thank you's and went on with daily life."

More than a year passed. Linda gave birth to her fifth child, and the other family's quilts were all but forgotten. However, in December she received a Christmas card from them. "There was a picture on the card of a very cute puppy and kitten," she describes. "The twins' mother worked for the Humane Society, and this was their fund-raising card. In the background of the photograph I saw something that kind of rang a bell, but I wasn't sure what it was."

An accompanying note jogged her memory. The family hoped Linda wouldn't mind that the Humane Society had chosen her red and green quilt as a backdrop for the card's animal photo.

Of course she didn't mind. Seeing her quilt on the card was a great compliment to her work, as valuable as all the "thank-you's" she'd received earlier. "I took the card to my quilt club's party that night and showed it to everyone. They were all very excited for me, and about five of them ordered Humane Society Christmas cards for the next year!"

The Quilting Frame: Linda's generous spirit brings to light Proverbs 11:25: "A generous man will prosper; he who refreshes others will himself be refreshed." The good deeds that she shares with others cause her to take hold "of the life that is *truly* life" (1 Timothy 6:18–19).

God's Template: "Now he who supplies seed to the sower and bread for food will also supply and increase your store of seed and will enlarge the harvest of your righteousness.

"You will be made rich in every way so that you can be generous on every occasion, and through us your generosity will result in thanksgiving to God.

"This service that you perform is not only supplying the needs of God's people but is also overflowing in many expressions of thanks to God.

"Because of the service by which you have proved yourselves, men will praise God for the obedience that accompanies your confession of the gospel of Christ, and for your generosity in sharing with them and with everyone else.

"And in their prayers for you their hearts will go out to you, because of the surpassing grace God has given you" (2 Corinthians 9:10–14).

The Binding Stitch: Thanks be to God for Your indescribable gift! You provide both seed and harvest for an abundant life.

Scrap Bag: When purchasing needles, consider smaller, rather than larger ones. Many quilters prefer sizes eight or nine "betweens." Some skillful quilters say they can make smaller stitches with smaller needles.

One Quilt, Forty-two Daughters

Phyllis Hoffman has more family photo albums than anyone else in her neighborhood. And now she has a family album quilt to go with them.

Ten years earlier, when she and her husband heard about Japanese college students coming to Spokane for a semester of English study, they volunteered to be host parents. The Hoffmans, a retired couple, picked up their first two host daughters and immediately fell in love with them. They introduced the girls to American life. They took them to the mall, to the park, and to church. In turn, their new "daughters" introduced the Hoffmans to a sampling of Japanese food, lessons in origami (paper-folding), and a deep appreciation for a different culture.

Within a semester or two, the Hoffmans realized they wanted to continue indefinitely as host parents, and they devised a plan to keep up with their growing family of Japanese daughters. First, they bought an album for each set of two host daughters. The album would contain photos, mementos, letters–anything that would remind them of their time together. Second, Mrs. Hoffman made an album quilt. She pieced it checkerboard-style with authentic Japanese fabrics given by one host daughter. The lighter prints are perfect for the girls' signatures.

After a decade of hosting Japanese students, the Hoffmans are "parents" to forty-two young women. They lovingly point to their photo albums and recall special memories with the girls. And they point to the quilt at the foot of their bed. It bears such names as Akiko, Maki, Yuko, and Hiroko. It also reflects return visits from former host daughters, who have brought parents and even boyfriends to see their American home and sign the quilt. It's a beautiful reminder of a couple's hospitality and of the large "family" they have acquired over the years.

The Quilting Frame: Imagine the pleasure these young women share as they add their names to the Hoffmans's quilt. They are no longer simply tourists in a foreign country but have become beloved members in the bigger "family" of God's world. Jesus, the Son of God, once said that we should become like little children who easily demonstrate love, forgiveness, and trust in others. In Mark 9:37 (KJV), He said, "Whosoever shall receive one of such children in my name, receiveth me: and whosoever shall receive me, receiveth not me, but him that sent me." The Bible says when we receive Jesus, our names are written in God's family album called the "Book of Life."

God's Template: "It shall come to pass in the latter days that the mountain of the Lord's house shall be [firmly] established as the highest of the mountains and shall be exalted above the hills, and all nations shall flow to it" (Isaiah 2:2 AMPLIFIED).

The Binding Stitch: Lord, lead me to those who feel as strangers in the land that I might give them water to quench their thirst and love them in Your Name.

Scrap Bag: Quilts are good for many functions besides bedcovers. Use them as wall hangings, drape them over sofas and rocking chairs, or spread them over tables. If you use a quilt as a tablecloth, be sure to cover it with a thin plastic sheet (like a painter's drop-cloth) before sitting down for a meal. Spills happen!

Friendship Quilt

You'll never finish this thing."

That's what my friend Ray said when I asked for his signature for a friendship quilt. He looked at my stack of muslin pieces, cut and ready for people to sign. He looked at the countless brown and green triangles I planned to use between the signatures. He looked at the spools of thread, the sewing machine, the quilting frame. And he doubted.

"It's just too big a project for a busy person like you."

No stranger to sewing, Ray knew the amount of work involved. He foresaw my unfinished quilt, stored in a drawer for eternity, even as he reluctantly added his signature to a muslin piece.

But his discouraging words only spurred me on. I'd already pieced and quilted three full-size quilts, and I believed I could do another. Besides, this was a special project. My husband and I were moving to Texas and would likely never see most of our South Carolina friends again. I wanted something tangible as a memory of them.

I wanted to remember Jimmy, the Native American neighbor who lent us folding chairs when we moved to the area, waiting until our moving van arrived.

I wanted to remember Sok, the Cambodian refugee who spoke little English but worked with me as a preschool assistant.

I wanted to remember Shirley, my boss, who encouraged me to study sign language.

I wanted to remember Faith, our friend at Winthrop College, the only person I've known who majored in viola.

And, yes, I wanted to remember Ray, who took me to the hospital when I broke my ankle at work; who carried me (with my leg cast) piggyback down a mountain path when we went hiking with our summer camp children; who helped my husband and me pack for the move to Texas.

I would show him and any other doubters that I could indeed finish the quilt. Within a month after we settled in Texas, I got out the signature pieces and embroidered the names. Next, I pieced the quilt by machine and quilted it by hand—a three-month project. Finally, I took a photo of it to send to Ray.

"I hate to admit it," came his letter, "but you really did it! Congratulations!"

Yes, Ray, I did it. Now, not only do I have a beautiful bedcover, I also have a precious reminder of friends and neighbors who were special in my life.

The Quilting Frame: Jesus summed up all ten commandments and the laws of Leviticus by saying, "Love God and love your neighbor." Defining the term "neighbor" Jesus confirmed, "The one who shows mercy to the stranger in need is the one who loved his neighbor" (Luke 10:37, author's paraphrase).

God's Template: " 'I was hungry and you gave Me food; I was thirsty and you gave Me drink; I was a stranger and you took Me in. . . . ' Assuredly, I say to you, inasmuch as you did it to one of the least of these My brethren, you did it to Me" (Matthew 25:35, 40 NKJV)

The Binding Stitch: Lord, show me ways to love others with practical, life-sustaining attention.

Scrap Bag: Join a quilt group, where you can meet people

with similar interests. Most cities have quilting organizations. Even small towns may have quilters who meet regularly at a church or community center. If you can't find a group, why not start one? Put an ad in the newspaper classifieds, and you'll get some phone calls.

Long - Distance Friends

They've never met in person, but a woman in Pennsylvania and a woman in Louisiana have become good friends because of a tragedy in Oklahoma.

When Oklahoma City's Alfred R. Murrah Federal Building was bombed on April 19, 1995, the public recoiled in horror. In the aftermath, stories of individual grief covered newspapers' front pages. Citizens across the country heard about the loss of men, women, and children in the senseless tragedy.

Yet, amid the sorrow, grief, and horror, some positive stories emerged—stories of heroism, stories of individuals reaching out to help strangers, stories of people making connections where there were none before.

Such is the case of quilter Lynn Johnson of Jersey Shore,

Pennsylvania. A member of her Tiadaghton Quilt Guild, Barbara Spittler, organized an Angel Quilt project in memory of the Oklahoma City children who lost their lives. The project was so popular that Barbara broadened the scope to include all the bombing victims. Lynn drew the name of Lakesha Racquel Levy and made an Angel Quilt in her memory, sending it to Oklahoma City with dozens of others from her area.

Soon, Lynn received a letter from Lakesha's mother, Constance Favorite, in New Orleans. The woman sent a photo of herself with the Angel Quilt and included information about Lakesha, her only child, and the two-year-old son she'd left behind. Lynn was touched by the letter, and she and Mrs. Favorite began corresponding regularly. As the friendship developed, Lynn offered to stitch a memory quilt.

The Favorites sent boxes of clothing and other memorabilia to be included in the quilt. Sorting through those items was an emotional strain for Lynn. But, "Once I got past the tears," she says, "I was able to get to work."

She chose pictures, letters to the mother, report cards from school, a birth certificate, a diploma, and certificates from Louisiana and the White House. At the family's request, she also included photos of the bombing site. The photos and documents were photocopied onto transfer paper, then ironed onto fabric. Interspersed among the photos on the quilt were twenty-one butterflies–appliquéd, embroidered, or pieced–representing twenty-one years of life, and made from the young woman's clothing.

The forty-eight-by-seventy-four-inch quilt arrived in New Orleans just in time for what would have been Lakesha's twenty-third birthday. The response from the family was "rejoicing, crying, and more rejoicing," says Mrs. Favorite. She plans to give the quilt to her grandson when he's old enough to care for it properly. Thanks to that quilt and to a quilting friend in Pennsylvania, he won't likely forget his mother.

Lynn has been blessed in the process, too. "This woman and I still exchange letters and phone calls. It's not unusual for me to find a package in the mail occasionally with a small gift. We have formed a very lovely friendship over the years."

The Quilting Frame: Through their talents, Lynn and her
quilting friends found a way to help survivors of tragedy
hold on to remnants of truth that will bring them future
strength. God has given all of us the ability to lift others
when they are down. As we, one-by-one, use our talents
to bring restoration and life to others, their mourning
will be turned to gladness again.

God's Template: "Hear, O LORD, and be merciful to me; O LORD, be my help. You turned my wailing into dancing; you removed my sackcloth and clothed me with joy, that my heart may sing to you and not be silent. O LORD my God, I will give you thanks forever" (Psalm 30:10–12).

The Binding Stitch: The LORD, Our God has been gracious in leaving us a remnant and giving us a firm place in Your sanctuary; You give light to our eyes and a little relief in our bondage (Ezra 9:8).

Scrap Bag: Use a properly fitting thimble. Even if you've never worn a thimble for other sewing projects, you'll want to use one for quilting. Be patient with yourself as you practice. Remember, quilting is a fine skill that must be learned. A thimble will help you become more skillful.

Love Bears

Since 1996, I've received dozens of letters from a woman I have never met, never spoken to, never heard of before. Only recently I learned she's a quilter.

In her first letter, she introduced herself as Ruth Glover of North Richland Hills, Texas. She had heard my name on a telephone prayer chain, and she wrote to assure me of her prayers for me and my church. I answered, thanking her and promising to keep her posted with regular church newsletters.

And so it began—a continuing correspondence across two thousand miles. Over the years, we've exchanged pictures. I sent one of me and my husband standing near our new church building. She sent one of herself sitting on the living room sofa. I replied with a photo of our Japanese host daughters visiting the church.

A few years into our pen-pal relationship, Mrs. Glover happened to mention that she enjoys quilting. The accompanying photograph of a full-size cathedral window quilt illustrated the point. Of course, my next letter to her included pictures of my recent projects. From then on, we swapped quilt stories along with prayer requests.

In one letter she asked, rather casually, if our church had a nursery. Are there babies and toddlers? Do they come regularly? I answered her questions, thinking she wanted the information so she could pray for our little ones.

The surprise came in a box delivered to the church just before Christmas. In it was a cathedral window baby quilt, with instructions to use it in our nursery. Each tiny "window" contained cute print fabric suitable for children—puppies, kittens, toy cars and locomotives, dolls, and flowers. I presented the quilt to the whole church on Christmas Sunday, on behalf of Mrs. Glover.

In her Christmas card, Mrs. Glover mentioned her special trademark, which I pointed out to the congregation: near the top of the quilt, four "windows" contained alphabet bears. Each of the bears had a different letter emblazoned on its shirt, and together they spelled LOVE. Mrs. Glover said her "Love Bears" are there to remind the children that Jesus loves them. "Always as I quilt I think of the babies whose lives I might touch through this. Wish I knew how many I have made, but I love to give them to churches for nurseries."

Mrs. Glover, nearly ninety years old, must remain at home

now due to poor health. She can't be as actively involved in church as she'd like. She can't visit sick or needy people; she can't teach Sunday school; she can't attend missionary meetings.

But she can pray. Her prayer support is vitally important to our church.

And, she can quilt. Her quilt is a visible reminder to our church of a faithful woman who uses her talents for the Lord.

The Quilting Frame: Quilting offers quiet solitude that is sometimes needed to hear the voice of the Lord. The Lord once spoke a message for all of us to Jeremiah, saying, "The thoughts that I think toward you are thoughts of peace and not of evil, to give you a future and a hope. So call upon Me and pray to Me, and I will listen to you. You will find Me when you search for Me with all your heart" (chapter 29:11–13, author's paraphrase).

God's Template: Jesus said, "Until now you have asked nothing in My name. Ask, and you will receive, that your joy may be full" (John 16:24 NKJV).

The Binding Stitch: Lord, thank You for listening to my prayers and granting the desires of my heart (Psalm 37:4).

Scrap Bag: If you've never made a quilt, you'd be wise to choose a small project first. Even when done on machine, a full-size bed quilt takes a long time, and the work may be daunting. It would be better to make a baby quilt, place mats, pot holders, or a wall hanging first, just to get a feel for the amount of work involved.

The Church Quilt

Irene called her longtime friend, Lola, to tell her that she had just heard Lola's son, Ed, preach at her church in Irving, Texas. Ed had traveled from Vancouver, Washington, with his wife, Nicky, to fill in for Irene's absent pastor.

"You must be proud of your son," Irene told Lola. "I want to make that boy a quilt with churches on it! Can you help by finding pictures to appliqué?"

Lola agreed and gathered photographs with family significance. Eager to begin, Irene made two appliquéd blocks, using phototransfers of Lola's pictures.

Then tragedy struck. Irene's husband Paul died suddenly, leaving her alone and grieving. She abandoned the quilt project, instead focusing her energies on funeral arrangements and the crisis of adjusting to life without her beloved husband.

After a time, good memories of Paul began filling her mind again. She remembered the day he had helped her shop for fabric for Ed and Nicky's quilt. He enjoyed the hunt as much as she did. They found prints to represent wood, brick, sky, and grass. Paul's enthusiasm always made Irene believe that her efforts were worthwhile.

Suddenly, she felt impressed to work on the church quilt again. As she pulled the finished blocks and unfinished pieces out of the sack she could almost hear Paul's voice saying, *"Good work, honey. This quilt will help that young pastor remember important people and places in his walk with God."*

Irene was inspired anew. Soon, she was ready to set the blocks together. Lola encouraged her friend with a gift of delightful beige-on-white fabric with tiny church buildings, which Irene used for sashing.

When Irene and Lola heard that Ed and Nicky would have a layover in the Dallas–Fort Worth Airport after a business trip, they knew it would be a perfect opportunity present their gift. They bundled up the quilt, battled the Dallas traffic, and located the correct airport terminal. After hellos and hugs, Lola and Irene unfolded the queen-size quilt.

Ed and Nicky were stunned with surprise. Finally Nicky exclaimed, "Ed, that's the church where we were married!"

"And," Ed rebounded with equal excitement, "over there's the church where I preached my first sermon!"

Lola pointed out the picture of the church where Ed's great-great grandmother was baptized in Germany. Through Nicky's and Ed's reactions, Irene could see their pleasure as fond memories came alive.

Traveling companions chimed in with their exclamations, and soon scores of people crowded around the display. Ooh's and aah's were standard among observers, while Lola and Irene repeatedly explained the origin of the quilt and the significance of the blocks. Ed and Nicky proudly toted the quilt home, and it graces their bed today.

Irene smiles when she recalls the story of how the bustling concourse at Dallas–Fort Worth International Airport came to a standstill one day because of a quilt.

The Quilting Frame: Good memories of those who have empowered our lives should inspire us to invest in others, to give freely as we have freely received. In Old Testament stories, stones of remembrance were placed as altars when God wanted His people to remember milestones of provision. When other generations passed by and saw the pile of stones, God knew they would ask, "What happened here?" Today, instead of building stone altars of remembrance, God sometimes whispers to one of us, "Make a quilt."

God's Template: "Finally, brothers, whatever is true, whatever is noble, whatever is right, whatever is pure, whatever is lovely, whatever is admirable—if anything is excellent or praiseworthy—think about such things" (Philippians 4:8).

The Binding Stitch: I will keep my mind on You, Lord, and in trusting You I know that I will have perfect peace (Isaiah 26:3).

Scrap Bag: Take at least two pictures of each quilt you make—one showing the whole quilt (as flat as possible) and the other showing a close-up of one block. Keep these photos in a safe place, as a record of your work. For a more extensive record, compile a scrapbook with photos, fabric samples, and other pertinent information.

Words Have Power

Two youngsters are depicted on Susan Leslie Lumsden's quilt. One is happy, smiling, skipping through a joyful childhood. The other is distressed, shameful, huddling in sorrow and despair. A close look at the geometric quilt reveals a reason for the contrasting demeanors:

Words.

Susan's quilt, a thirty-by-forty-one-inch wall hanging, is titled "The Power of the Spoken Word," and it illustrates the importance of affirmation over criticism in a child's life. A border of appliquéd handprints surrounds the quilt, half of which is a colorful array of concentric triangles with the happy child in the middle. All strips of the triangles contain handwritten words of encouragement. Examples include "What is your idea about this?" and "Your work is important to me."

Susan chose this design for a reason. "I used the triangle," she says, "to show the firm foundation and strength of the affirming word, because a triangle is the strongest structure in nature."

By contrast, the distressed child is relegated to one small corner of the other half of the quilt, where strips of fabric containing bitter and unkind phrases are aimed at him. "You're just like your father, and I divorced him" and "There's no hope for you; I give up," are two heartbreaking examples.

This portion of the design also has a purpose. "I deliberately had the flow of words going toward the abused child, making him smaller and isolated. That's what verbal abuse does—introverts, isolates, and destroys self-esteem."

Many people consider child abuse only in the realm of extreme physical acts, but Susan believes words can also be abusive. "I wanted to convey the idea that what is said to a child can be just as scarring as physical damage. All too often one hears things said that absolutely chill one to the bone in view of the potential damage."

Susan was one of twenty-eight persons who made quilts in response to an Internet challenge from Quiltart. All of their quilts can be seen on the Internet. The actual collection is on a worldwide tour, educating people about the dangers of child abuse.

The positive side of Susan's quilt holds special meaning for her. In her own life, she says, while making the quilt, "I came to the delightful conclusion that although I had many disagreements with my parents as a teen, I never was truly abused." She remembers her parents' words of encouragement as an important part of her childhood. She notes, "Do people realize how valuable a well-timed praise or a simple hug and 'I love you' can be? Knowing you are special can make all the difference."

The Quilting Frame: Our hearts are often like the two-sided quilt. We try to do good, but selfishness tempts us to disregard the feelings of others. Sometimes, we aren't even kind to ourselves. King David lamented in Psalm 64:3 that some people "sharpen their tongues like swords and aim their words like deadly arrows." We have no power over the self-centered nature within us, and no protection against fiery darts aimed our way, but God's words are life to us, and He is our shield, Who lifts our head, and gives us the power to do what is right (see Psalm 3:3; 2 Samuel 22:36). We need only to ask for His help.

God's Template: "The mind of sinful man is death, but the

mind controlled by the Spirit is life and peace"
(Romans 8:6).

*The Binding Stitch: May the words of my mouth and the medita-
tion of my heart be pleasing in Your sight, O LORD, my
Rock and my Redeemer* (Psalm 19:14).

Scrap Bag: When setting blocks together for a quilt top, it's
sometimes difficult to decide on the best arrangement.
You could lay them out on a bed, a table, or the floor,
but you won't be looking at them from a good angle.
It's better to have a flannel wall. Use a large piece of
flannel, tacked to a wall. Press your quilt blocks onto
the flannel, and they'll stay until you're ready to move
them. You can view your arrangement from across the
room and get an accurate impression of the future
quilt top.

A Generous Friend

Jessica and her teenage daughter Ashley know that generosity can travel full circle.

Jessica had started a quilt for Ashley, incorporating the girl's favorite colors and patterns. She finished piecing the top but couldn't find the time to quilt it. Meanwhile, Ashley's school band decided to raise money for new uniforms by having a quilt raffle.

Jessica approached Ashley with her idea. "Honey, I'd like to donate this quilt of yours to the raffle. I'll make you another one really soon. What do you think?" After a moment's hesitation, Ashley agreed, knowing the fund-raiser was important. Jessica found someone who could machine-quilt, and the donation was soon ready.

The raffle was a huge success. People throughout the community bought tickets, including Debbie, one of Jessica's co-workers.

Debbie bought six tickets, and one of them was the winner. That should have been the end of the story, but Debbie had another idea.

After getting the call informing her of the win, Debbie requested that Ashley herself deliver the prize. When Ashley arrived carrying the quilt, she told Debbie, "You won! It's yours! They drew your name."

"Maybe they drew my name," Debbie replied, grinning, "but it's not my quilt. It's yours. I'm giving it back to you."

Stunned, Ashley accepted the quilt, realizing that most people would not have been so generous. After all, the quilt *was* Debbie's. But Debbie knew the time and effort Jessica had put into the quilt. She wanted Ashley to have it.

Ashley now enjoys the quilt at college, always remembering that it was twice given and twice received. Generosity sometimes pays back in double rewards.

The Quilting Frame: Jesus once said, "It is better to give than to receive." He knew God promised that we would reap what we sow, and He dared us to test God and see the wonderful harvest that giving would bring. "Give," He said, "and it will be given to you. A good measure, pressed down, shaken together and running over, will be poured into your lap. For with the measure you use, it will be measured to you" (Luke 6:38).

God's Template: " 'Bring the whole tithe into the storehouse, that there may be food in my house. Test me in this,' says the LORD Almighty, 'and see if I will not throw open the floodgates of heaven and pour out so much blessing that you will not have room enough for it' " (Malachi 3:10).

The Binding Stitch: Thank You, Lord, that You do not withhold the secret to happiness; You have taught us to give, and You even supply us with the seed to sow.

Scrap Bag: The finishing touch to a quilt is its binding. Many quilters choose to make bias binding; others prefer straight. Bias binding may be better for quilts whose edges have lots of curves or points. Straight binding is often preferred for straight-edged quilts. The color of binding depends on the color and mood of the quilt. Some bindings are black, as if to frame the quilt formally. Others are scrappy, pieced to complement a scrap quilt. Still others are the same color as the back of the quilt.

Grandmother's Stars

The package arrived unexpectedly, and when I opened it I found the beginnings of a three-generation quilt.

My sister Jean, living in Florida, had prepared for a move and wanted to reduce her supply of household clutter. One such item was a forgotten box she found in the back of a closet. It contained scraps of fabric and envelopes filled with quilt patterns. Not a quilter herself, she decided to mail the box to me.

I'm glad she did.

Her note indicated that she'd inherited the box from Mother years earlier, who'd gotten some of the stuff from Grandma a decade or so before that. As I unfolded the paper patterns, I discovered a Dutch girl for appliqué, a miniature basket for a six-inch block, and a simple diamond for an eight-pointed star. Digging deeper, I found a collection of diamond-shaped calico pieces among heaps of assorted scraps. I also found four fabric stars already pieced from the diamonds, alternating with prints and solids.

These stars exhibited different styles of sewing. Two of them were pieced with a single strand of white thread, and the other two with a double strand of beige thread. The first two stars had close, even stitches; the others' stitches were tiny but not as even. Perhaps the four stars were done by two different women—one with a steady hand, the other less steady.

Jean and I surmised that Grandma Lowry had begun a Scrappy Star quilt but never finished it. Then, we imagined, Mother took over but for some reason couldn't complete the project, either. Now it was my turn. Would I be willing to finish a job begun more than half a century earlier?

I decided to give it a try. My husband and I were approaching a summer vacation, so I gathered needle, thread, thimble, and the fabric diamonds to take on the road. At every opportunity I pieced stars, finishing dozens of them before returning home. I then cut more diamonds from the scraps in the box, to make enough stars to complete the quilt top. Next was the chore of appliquéing them onto muslin, then stitching a multicolored border with the remaining scraps. I quilted it simply, with straight diagonal lines connecting the stars. Sending a photo to Jean confirmed that I had indeed closed the loop. The Lowry-McHaney-Danner quilt was finished at last.

The Quilting Frame: We shouldn't let unfinished projects overwhelm us. Perhaps some of our projects are supposed to remain unfinished, so that we might inspire some daughter of a future generation to copy our work and carry on the vital arts. The Lord empowered King Solomon to construct the temple that his father David dreamed of building. The completion of London's Westminster Abbey took hundreds of years. Each generation somehow received inspiration to continue on with the worthwhile projects that their ancestors began. Time is not an obstacle for plans ordained by God.

God's Template: "My father David had it in his heart to build a temple for the Name of the LORD, the God of Israel. But the LORD said to my father David, 'Because it was in your heart to build a temple for my Name, you did well to have this in your heart. Nevertheless, you are not the one to build the temple, but your son, who is your own flesh and blood—he is the one who will build the temple for my Name' " (2 Chronicles 6:7–9).

The Binding Stitch: Lord, give me wisdom to see what is vital, courage to let go of the rest.

Scrap Bag: What color should your quilting thread be? Many quilters prefer white or off-white, which is the norm for a traditional look. Others like the quilting thread to match the color of the fabric being quilted, so they may use several colors of quilting thread in one quilt. Still others may want a contrasting color, to highlight the quilting. You might even find metallic thread appealing, which gives an exotic look to the finished quilt. Before you buy, decide whether you'll be quilting by machine or by hand, then be sure the thread is appropriate for your use.

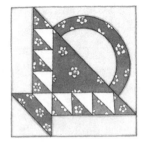

World's Worst Quilt

Even expert quilters have disasters in their past.

Such is the case with Ellen Sherriffs, a member of the Washington State Quilters. She made her first quilt years ago without any knowledge of the subject, without any instruction or guidance. "I just thought it would be fun!" she remembers.

Much of her work on that quilt represented a departure from the norm. For example, "I figured if a little batting was good, a lot would be better. But, I didn't have quite enough for a double layer for the entire quilt." There's an overall lumpiness, she says, which most quilts don't have. Other unique features included dark thread stitching light fabrics, and poorly sewn seams coming apart to reveal leaky batting.

When, after three years, she finished the quilt, she read about Ami Simms's World's Worst Quilt Contest in a magazine. "I knew

I had to enter this quilt. My husband helped me take pictures of it to include with the entry form." They tried to photograph the quilt from several angles, in hopes of convincing the judges of its worthiness. "We got all of the mismatched seams, the chopped off blocks, the ripple in the middle where it's not quite flat."

Then they had to write a brief description of why this should be considered the world's worst quilt. With the proverb "honesty is the best policy" running through their heads, they admitted to the judges that the quilt had more going for it than just poor construction. Every animal they'd owned in those three years had used it for a bed and bathroom. It had been washed and rewashed repeatedly and already had seen more wear than many quilts do over a lifetime.

"The judges liked our reasoning," Ellen says, "and they asked me to send them the quilt." Her entry didn't win the competition, but Ami Simms photographed it to use as part of her lecture tour. After the contest, Ami said in an interview that she wasn't surprised at the truly awful quilts people had created. But she was surprised that people had kept them.

"I can understand that," agrees Ellen, "but I treat this quilt as carefully as I treat my more beautiful creations. It's very warm and reminds me how much I've learned." However, remembering her pets' use of the quilt in its earlier days, she says, "I just don't put it on the top of the bed because I don't want the cats or dog to see it."

The Quilting Frame: If we live without God's wisdom, our lives soon resemble Ellen's old quilt. Some of the corners we had carefully cut don't match up, and unwelcome critters soon nest in the folds of our remaining charm. We can wash and rewash our lives, but nothing gets rid of the overall lumpiness of our unprofessional attempt to make something of ourselves. Then Jesus graciously offers to exchange our old life for His new one. "You can wear My robe of righteousness," He offers, "and I have a perfect place to keep your old quilt."

God's Template: "But ask the Lord Jesus Christ to help you live as you should" (Romans 13:14 TLB).

The Binding Stitch: Thank You, Lord, for removing the blanket of my sins as far away from me as the east is from the west (Psalm 103:12).

Scrap Bag: Think twice before throwing that quilt in the washing machine! Many older quilts won't hold up well, even in the gentle cycle. Rather, you might consider soaking a soiled quilt in a bathtub full of warm water, using a gentle cleanser. After the quilt has soaked, let the water drain out and fill the tub again, without removing the quilt. Repeat the process until the water is clear. Then, drain the tub and press the quilt (don't wring) to remove excess water. Lift the quilt out and spread it on a clean sheet in the back-yard, away from dogs and direct sunlight, if possible. Allow several hours for quilt to dry.

St. Pat's Quilts

Apples, spaceships, schoolhouses, sunflowers—each is a cute idea for a quilt pattern. Put a child's photo with it and you've got a winning combination.

That's what Becky Clift and Lisa Chan have discovered. Both are primary teachers at St. Patrick's School in Spokane. In their spare time they make quilts for the school's fundraising auctions.

For each of the past ten years Becky and her mother, Donna Senkler, have designed a quilt, and Donna has pieced it. Most of the quilts' patterns resembled St. Pat's children in their uniforms. The quilts were always popular items at the auction, where bidding would increase far beyond the actual cost of labor and materials.

Three years ago Lisa joined in and began making her own quilts for the auction. Her first consideration was the bottom line:

"What kind of quilt can I make that'll raise the most money?"

After looking at dozens of patterns, contemporary and traditional, she decided on bold, bright sunflowers. To make the flowers even more attractive, she thought, why not put a child's picture in the center of each one? She chose members of her kindergarten class, posing individually for their school pictures.

Lisa's husband, Gen, used a computer to scan the pictures and print them onto the fabric. Each cloth photo was then cut to the proper size, and the sunflowers were completed. This first effort of Lisa's was a huge success at the auction, drawing bids higher than she had hoped. The following year she made a similar quilt, with pictures of children looking out the windows of rocketships.

Becky, too, saw the popularity of the photo quilts. In recent years she's used her first graders' school pictures on her quilts. She takes the pictures to a copy shop and has them printed onto fabric. Her mother then adds them to the design. One quilt pattern was a collection of schoolhouses with open doors revealing children's faces. Her most recent creation was a quilt of apples, with a child's face in each apple. Embroidered phrases, such as "An apple for the teacher," were interspersed as well. The quilt is machine-quilted, with ornate stippling around the apples.

Becky's and Lisa's quilts are among the auction's hottest items. After all, who wouldn't want a beautiful, lifelong reminder of grade school friends?

The Quilting Frame: The joyful faces of children peering through open doors and windows on the quilt are a fresh reminder of Jesus' words, "I tell you the truth, unless you change [turn about] and become like little children [trusting, lowly, loving, forgiving], you will never enter the kingdom of heaven" (Matthew 18:3). We are to train children in the way they should go, keeping with their individual gifts (Proverbs 22:6), but during their lessons we are to learn their ways so that our countenance will shine through open doors, too.

God's Template: "If I say, I will forget my complaint, I will put off my sad countenance, and be of good cheer and brighten up" (Job 9:27 AMPLIFIED).

The Binding Stitch: "I was young and now I am old, yet I have never seen the righteous forsaken or their children begging bread. They are always generous and lend freely; their children will be blessed" (Psalm 37:25–26).

Scrap Bag: Subscribe to a quilt magazine. You'll find several on the market. A magazine coming into your home every month, full of color pictures and instructions, will keep your interest high and inspire you to continue your quilting projects.

Help from Many Hands

The traditional picture of the quilting bee includes American women in pioneer dresses, sitting around a quilt frame. But today's bee may look quite different, and the women holding the needles may not even be American.

Each semester, 150–200 students from Mukogawa Women's University in Japan arrive in Spokane, Washington, and settle into fourteen weeks of American life for their studies-abroad program. The faculty here try to instill in their students some special aspects of America which can't easily be learned from books. One example is quilting. Instructors Tim White and Gregg Brekke developed a unit of study called "The Spirit of the American West." Some of their objectives were to experience the sociability of quilting bees and to create a community quilt project. Tim and Gregg approached quilter

Susan Thompson, Mukogawa's library media specialist, for help.

"I suggested that each group of students produce small quilts rather than a large one. After brainstorming, we decided that if every student made one nine-inch block, we could put them together into baby quilts." They also decided to donate the finished quilts to a local women and children's shelter. "Every baby," says Susan, "should have one warm blanket, and the idea of donating just seemed right." They hoped by this project to teach the students about friendship quilts given to pioneer families.

After Susan purchased supplies, Tim and Gregg cut squares and sashing for the nine-patch blocks and were ready when students arrived to sew. First, they taught the girls about seam size and stitch length, along with basic safety procedures. Then they gave them needles, thread, and fabric. "The students were encouraged to discuss things around the table, in English, as you would at an old-fashioned quilting bee," Susan explains. "This kept them working hard, and hopefully improving their English skills. Teachers circulated and checked on seam allowances and stitch length, as well as the right combination of light and dark patterns. Sometimes, teachers had to rip out mistakes and students had to start over." As each girl finished her nine-patch, she pressed it and signed the middle block with a fabric pen. Next, Susan set the blocks into quilt tops, and volunteers helped tie the layers together. In two semesters, 325 Japanese students made and signed blocks for twenty-seven baby quilts. The project had an impact on students as well as on the recipients of the quilts. Susan remembers, "The letters we teachers received from the shelter told about the appreciation of the mothers and children, and it gave us all a very nice, warm feeling that in teaching about something, we made a difference for someone else. The students went away from our class feeling good about the fact that something they did helped a great deal of people."

The Quilting Frame: When God teaches us something, it invariably changes us and impacts others. By being teachable we remain open to the leading of God's Holy Spirit to show us what He wants to do in us and through us. We are not designed to be reservoirs of God's love and blessings, but we are sent into the world to lead others to His rivers of living water, and to give freely to others what He has given to us.

God's Template: "Jesus stood and said in a loud voice, 'If anyone is thirsty, let him come to me and drink. Whoever believes in me, as the Scripture has said, streams of living water will flow from within him.'

"By this he meant the Spirit, whom those who believed in him were later to receive. Up to that time the Spirit had not been given, since Jesus had not yet been glorified" (John 7:37–39).

The Binding Stitch: I will follow in Your footsteps, Lord, that I may learn valuable lessons that can be passed on to others (1 Peter 2:21).

Scrap Bag: Do not eat or drink (except water) while you're quilting. You may spill something on the quilt. Or, your fingers may transfer food particles onto the quilt. Or, you may lick your finger before tying a knot in the thread, and that end of the thread will become stained with the color of the food or drink.

Good Intentions, Bad Process

No one realized the problem until it was too late.

Audrey had invited a few of her most trusted quilting friends to her home for a bee, a light lunch, and a few hours of cozy conversation. In exchange for a day of hospitality, we would quilt her newest creation—a beautiful, full-size black and white work of art designed by her architect granddaughter. Audrey planned to enter it in an upcoming competition.

She set up the quilting frame, a two-by-three-foot free-standing PVC structure. We draped the backing, batting, and quilt top over it like a layered tablecloth, then clamped it securely. With the center of the quilt stretched taut in the frame, four quilters sat around it.

"Where can I sit?"

"What about me?"

"Isn't there any more room?" the rest of us lamented.

Audrey's response made good sense: "You three sit just beyond the floor frame. Grab the quilt's loose edges and use your small lap frames. Just quilt whatever you can reach." And so we worked, finishing almost all of the quilt before leaving that day.

We didn't see Audrey again until the next month, when she told us the problem we'd created. It seemed that we on the edges had not been able to quilt continuously. That is, we'd left areas unquilted between our small frames and the larger floor frame. "Gaps!" she moaned. "Gaps and puckers whenever I quilted those areas!" Fortunately, her scolding was good-natured. "I stayed awake two days and nights, taking out all of your stitches around the edges. I requilted everything but the middle!"

The extra work was necessary, of course, if the quilt was to be competitive in the contest. And we who had done the original quilting were sorry for Audrey. We regretted our attempt to shortcut the process. All of us knew that continuous quilting is better than leaving gaps to be quilted later, yet we doggedly worked on, hoping that somehow it would turn out all right. Our intentions were good, but our process was flawed.

In our human efforts we often try to find shortcuts—ways to make life easier. This isn't always bad; some of our greatest inventions are the results. But when the process is crucial, and any variation will cause problems, we should avoid the shortcuts. In Audrey's case, hours of rework were necessary because we bypassed the correct process. She barely finished the quilt it time for the competition. At the next bee, we'll be more careful.

The Quilting Frame: Even the best intentions can be ruined by a faulty process. The Old Testament Book of Judges, chapters 13–16, tells of Samson, who was given super-natural strength by God. Unfortunately, Samson often used his gift from God simply to satisfy his own desires. His self-serving actions resulted in betrayal by his wife and blindness inflicted by his enemies. This caused him untold suffering and humiliation. Finally, though, Samson made a choice that followed God's way instead of his own. In turning back to the Lord, he defeated his opponents.

God's Template: "But do not forget this one thing, dear friends: With the Lord a day is like a thousand years, and a thousand years are like a day. The Lord is not slow in keeping his promise, as some understand slowness. He is patient with you, not wanting anyone to

perish, but everyone to come to repentance"
(2 Peter 3:8–9).

The Binding Stitch: When we look for shortcuts, Lord, help us to remember that You would wait a thousand years for us to do the right thing.

Scrap Bag: Always begin quilting from the center, working toward the edges. Quilt continuously, smoothing out ripples on the back as you go.

Warmth around the World

The Sunshine Quilt Project has impacted countless people in need. It's the joint effort of several Internet groups, comprising over six hundred men and women who donate time, talents, and energies to send warmth and hugs around the world. Friends of the on-line Sunshine Project recruit off-line help from scouting troops, senior adults centers, schools, and churches to make and donate bed-covers. Coordinators Billijean Hobson (Sunshine Quilt Group) and Bev Bennett (Mystery Quilters) and their volunteers ship the quilts to the International Red Cross. As many as fifteen hundred quilts are shipped each year. In most cases, Sunshine never hears from the recipients.

One time they did.

Through an unusual set of circumstances, a Sunshine volunteer met an Albanian exchange student at a Rotary Club luncheon. The eighteen-year-old girl had a name that was difficult to pronounce. But since she represents many who receive Sunshine quilts, we'll call her "Sunny" in this account. During the meal, the Americans asked questions about Sunny's homeland. Conversation centered around Albania until the Americans noticed a change in her demeanor. She grew sad, forlorn, maybe homesick. They decided to cheer her up by changing the subject.

The Sunshine volunteer took the lead. "I thought I'd tell the story of our quilts, a very upbeat topic! I mentioned that we send them to the International Red Cross, and from there they are distributed wherever needed the most."

At that point, Sunny began crying and left her seat. "She came over to hug me," says the volunteer. "When she was composed enough to talk she said 'Thank you' over and over. Then she explained that she'd seen so many people freezing that it hurt to think about it. She remembered seeing 'pretty new blankets' made with 'little pieces,' but not understanding where they'd come from."

A blanket made of little pieces can indeed touch the heart. It can warm a person physically as well as emotionally. Sunny and thousands of others like her around the world know this, thanks to the Sunshine Quilt Project.

The Quilting Frame: The account of Jesus' meeting with Zacchaeus, in Luke 19:1–10, shows that God cares about our emotional sense of self-worth. Zacchaeus was hated and snubbed by the townspeople, but Jesus chose to honor him by calling out his name and visiting his house. This personal attention caused Zacchaeus to change from a selfish to a generous neighbor. Sunshine filled Zacchaeus's house that day, just as it must have filled the hearts of those who received the Project's quilts.

God's Template: "For the Son of Man came to seek and to save what was lost" (Luke 19:10).

The Binding Stitch: Cause me to see those who need light in their moments of darkness, and show me how to warm their hearts with Your love, Lord.

Scrap Bag: Many instruments are available for marking quilting lines. You may use chalk, chalk pencils, disappearing markings, water-soluble markings or quilters' masking tape. If you use the purple disappearing marker, remember that the quilting lines you draw will be gone in a few hours. Plan to mark only the area you'll have time to quilt that day.

Farmwoman and Quilter

A few miles from Cleburne, Texas, stands a little farmhouse, alone on a quiet road. It's the house Seby Rosser built for his bride, Joy, in about 1920. It's not an architectural masterpiece, nor is it worthy of a full-color layout in a home and garden magazine.

It's just a white frame house with a couple of bedrooms, and porches on front and back that overlook cattle grazing in surrounding pastures.

It's a house where quilts were made.

Joy Rosser married Seby when she was sixteen, and he erected the house a couple of years later. Her life was a busy one. She did chores with Seby on their dairy farm; she kept a garden and preserved the produce; she reared six children and participated in church activities.

All this was typical of a farm wife in those days. But Joy went beyond typical. As her name implies, she liked to have fun as well. She set up a playground in her backyard for neighboring children. In it were a trolley ride (cable and pulleys strung between trees), a merry-go-round (large buggy wheel), a see-saw, a swing, and a basketball hoop. She soon realized those children didn't attend church, so she began weekly Bible studies in her yard, inviting everyone within walking distance to the "class," then offering refreshments and games afterward. She made her own visual aids, providing illustrations of Bible stories for each child to take home.

In her spare time, after the chores, after the games, after the Bible lessons, she pieced and quilted—also typical of a busy farm wife in the 1920s. But, like herself, Joy's quilts were beyond typical. Rather than use traditional patterns, Joy drafted her own designs.

"If I see a pretty picture in the newspaper, or a cartoon I like, or a flower by the roadside, I'll draw it up and make it into a quilt," she explained. "I've made so many quilts with just my own patterns, that I've pretty near lost count of 'em."

Indeed, her quilts are unique. One remarkable creation is a nearly life-size appliqué of Dallas Cowboys football player Tony Dorsett running with a football. She made it for a fund-raiser for her grandson's high school band. It brought five hundred dollars, publicity from Dallas television and newspapers, and a face-to-face meeting with Mr. Dorsett himself.

She also made a quilt which interests local historians. It's filled with embroidered drawings of old buildings in and around Cleburne, including houses, the courthouse, a depot, and a church building, some of which no longer exist. She made her sketches on fabric from a collection of local postcards and calendars.

The children are all grown now, with children and grandchildren of their own. Joy Rosser passed away in the mid-1990s, but her memory lives on. Before her death, she designated each of her quilts for a specific offspring, and now scores of Rosser descendants have their own legacy of Joy.

The Quilting Frame: King Solomon said that God planted a sense of purpose in our hearts and minds, so that nothing can satisfy us but to find God's plan for our lives. God repeatedly calls us to love Him, love others, and enjoy the fruit of our labor. Joy Rosser used her hands to do good for others and thus enjoyed the greatest pleasure under the sun.

God's Template: "Moreover, when God gives any man wealth and possessions, and enables him to enjoy them, to accept his lot and be happy in his work—this is a gift of God." (Ecclesiastics 5:19).

Binding Stitch: When I put my trust in You, Lord, You keep me occupied with gladness of heart (Ecclesiastics 5:20).

Scrap Bag: Lap quilting appeals to busy people who don't have time to sit at a quilt frame. If you want to do a large, hand-quilted project, you might want to consider lap quilting. Make each block as if it were a tiny quilt, by piecing, layering, and basting it together, then quilting it on a small lap frame. Don't quilt all the way to the edges, though. You'll want to join the blocks together on their rough edges after they're quilted.

Quick Work

Want something organized in a hurry? Need to mobilize scores of people for immediate action? Quilters can do it!

Ann Turley of Walnut, California, knows this to be true. She saw her quilt guild shift into high gear and put together a beautiful quilt in record time, for a good cause. In this case, the good cause was Ann herself.

After a biopsy, Ann learned the distressing news: a lumpectomy would be required to remove a tumor. But that wasn't sufficient. "A few days later the doctor told me he couldn't get it all," Ann explains, "so I would need a mastectomy."

By now, a friend in Ann's quilt group, the TLC Quilters of West Covina, had heard the news. This woman, along with a second friend, galvanized the others with a last-minute insert in their guild's monthly paper. The note explained the situation and requested signed quilt blocks from as many as possible, as quickly as possible. In fact, when members received the newsletter, they had only two days to piece a block, sign it, and bring it to the guild meeting.

Such short notice often results in meager participation, but not so with the TLC group. Sixty-four women responded, interrupting their regular routines to make six-inch Irish chain blocks and write words of encouragement on them. Meanwhile, the organizers of the project were also making blocks–thirty-six of them–for the border. The sixty-four blocks arrived on schedule, and the two leaders worked night and day to set them together. Quilting was done by several in the group, and the finished product was presented to Ann. From conception to completion, the quilt took just a couple of weeks.

Ann recalls, "It was a total surprise. The two quilters showed up on my doorstep the evening before my mastectomy to give me the quilt. I was absolutely speechless! How could any guild manage to pull a quilt together in such a short amount of time?"

The surprise was even sweeter to Ann as she read the messages on the blocks. Some were humorous, some serious. Several included passages of Scripture, causing her to affirm, "God is not dead in the quilting community!" The speed of the project and the outpouring of love made a profound impression on her. "There were no words to express what I felt. I cried and laughed over this wonderful gift from my quilting friends."

Quilting Frame: Sometimes all we need to get well is an encouraging word and reassurance that we are loved. When Ann needed that hope, the TLC quilters were quick to send words of faith as well as their demonstration of love to her. When we needed hope, God sent His Word and His demonstration of love to us through Jesus.

God's Template: "In the beginning was the Word, and the Word was with God, and the Word was God. The Word became flesh and made his dwelling among us. We have seen his glory, the glory of the One and Only [Jesus], who came from the Father, full of grace and truth" (John 1:1, 14).

The Binding Stitch: "Ah, Lord God! Behold, You have made the heavens and the earth by Your great power and out stretched arm. There is nothing too hard for You" (Jeremiah 32:17 NKJV).

Scrap Bag: If you like small projects, buy a lap-size version of the PVC frame. You can take it apart quickly for carrying to a quilting bee. A round or half-round hoop can also serve well for a small quilt. It can be used on a stand or on the lap.

Angel Kitten

Dr. Susan Balter knows that chemotherapy can be eased a bit with the addition of quilt therapy. This physician/quilter has stitched bedcovers for several people with serious medical problems. She tells of one incident involving a colleague with lymphoma. The patient realized the seriousness of her illness as she faced the prospect of chemo treatments. Lymphoma can destroy a woman's ability to bear children and, in some cases, can take her life.

During this trying time winter hit the Midwest with a blast. One morning, when the temperature was below zero, Dr. Balter's friend discovered a tiny kitten huddled on her doorstep. She took him in and nursed him back to health. He was just the companion she needed, and she considered him a blessing from above. She called him her angel.

Dr. Balter describes the events that followed. "I made a quilt with an angel in the center and kittens around it. Then I had her colleagues and friends pen messages to her on the quilt in indelible ink." These special messages covered the quilt, including the areas surrounding the kittens and angel.

Soon it was time for the chemo treatments to begin. "The cancer center arranged for her to come early for that first chemotherapy," Dr. Balter says, "so that I might give her this quilt without other patients around. While she unwrapped it, they started her chemo infusion. I had the privilege of watching this young woman become so absorbed reading the messages that for forty-five minutes, she didn't know what was going on around her." Instead of worrying over the chemo, she spent the time twisting and turning the quilt and enjoying the sentiments from her friends.

The patient made it through chemotherapy and has more recently survived a bone marrow transplant. She is now married, and the angel kitten quilt adorns a wall in her home.

The Quilting Frame: Our faith should connect to the needs of others. Listening is an active part of our encouragement to others. While any quilt would have been a wonderful gift, Dr. Balter listened to her friend and knew the "angel kitten" quilt would speak specifically to the individual need of *this* patient. Its healing message communicated, "You are unique and valuable. God will send you kittens and friends and mercy in the form of a quilt to comfort you during your time of need."

God's Template: "Each one should use whatever gift he has received to serve others, faithfully administering God's grace in its various forms" (1 Peter 4:10).

The Binding Stitch: Cause me to pursue the things which make for peace and the building up of others (Romans 14:19 NASB).

Scrap Bag: All-cotton batting makes a cozier quilt than polyester, but it doesn't hold together as well. If you use a cotton batt, be sure to quilt it closely. Quilting lines should be no more than an inch apart. Larger gaps will result in bunched-up batting later in the life of the quilt.

Ink Blots

From the beginning I'd hoped to enter my Texas signature quilt in the county fair—maybe even in the state fair. It would be large (queen-size), patriotic (red, white, and blue), and eye-catching (a Texas-flag bandanna as the center medallion). I could envision it on display at the fair with a best-of-show ribbon pinned to its edge.

The work progressed as scheduled. In August I sent in the required entry forms. In September I quilted the final stitches, just two days before the judging. Lastly, I grabbed a spray bottle of water to erase the blue quilting lines.

As I sprayed, though, I realized with horror that some of the friendship signatures must have been written with non-permanent markers. Blue and black bled onto my beautiful white background. Within seconds, a half-dozen signatures smeared, and ugly blotches appeared on the quilt.

"Eeek! Oh, no! It's a disaster!" My husband heard my screams and rushed into the room. While I paced the floor, he calmly assessed the situation and took off for the drugstore, returning moments later with a half-dozen spot removers, each promising its own kind of miracle.

We followed instructions carefully, trying a different concoction on every spot, but nothing worked. The quilt was ruined. I let it dry, then folded it and put it in a closet. Gone were my dreams of a spectacular display at the fair. No best-of-show ribbon this year.

Weeks passed, and the emotional trauma subsided. That's when I braced myself to do something drastic. What did I have to lose? I'd never tried such a thing before, but with my sharpest scissors I nervously cut away a damaged block—top, batting, and backing—leaving a rectangular hole in the quilt. Next, I cut a new signature block and re-signed the name. I then cut another piece of batting and backing to fit, and stitched the new set into the hole. After quilting the area, I was surprised to find a presentable result. I tried the same technique with another signature, then another. Despair turned to relief, then joy, as I realized my work wasn't ruined after all.

The Texas quilt has never won a ribbon in a competition. It will, however, grace our bed for years to come. And it serves as a reminder of lessons learned. First, always use permanent marking pens when signing a quilt; and second, don't be afraid to try something drastic when normal efforts fail.

The Quilting Frame: God Himself uses drastic means sometimes to fix people's mistakes. The Old Testament Book of Jonah tells of how He chose a huge fish to swallow a man who had made the mistake of running from God. If God is willing to do such a dramatic thing, then I should be willing to try new ideas, too. When one method fails, I should attempt something different—maybe something I've never done before. The result could be a surprising success, like my reconstructed quilt blocks. What have I got to lose?

God's Template: "Have mercy on me, O God, according to your unfailing love; according to your great compassion blot out my transgressions. Wash away all my iniquity and cleanse me from my sin." (Psalm 51:1–2).

The Binding Stitch: Thank You for blotting out the stains of my wrongdoing, and cleansing the fabric of my life with Your unfailing love that makes all things new.

Scrap Bag: Most quilting and fabric shops have permanent marking pens, appropriate for signing friendship quilts. Make a test block first, with the same fabric you'll have in the whole quilt. Then wash and dry it to be sure of the pen's capabilities.

Legacy over the Years

DiAnn always imagined she would dread the day her daughter would announce her engagement, but to her relief she felt happy anticipation for the new life her grown-up child was about to enjoy. DiAnn wanted to find something significant to give Mary Christina that would speak of all the good that God intended for a marriage.

The choices of potential gifts began to overwhelm her, but nothing spoke of the divine "ideal" the institution of marriage upheld. One morning she began to speculate what it might have been like for her mother and her grandmother when they were at Mary Christina's place in life. *With fewer choices, greatness was more obvious*, she thought, and that is when DiAnn thought of the perfect gift for her daughter's bridal shower.

More than half a century earlier, DiAnn's mother had received two quilt tops as wedding gifts from her groom's grandmothers. One was a Double Wedding Ring pattern, and the other a Grandmother's Flower Garden. DiAnn remembered watching her mother fold them carefully and store them away for safekeeping, saying, "Someday I'll have them quilted."

DiAnn hoped that her mother still had the quilt tops, in spite of all the moves her parents had made since her childhood. When DiAnn called and asked about them, her mother seemed relieved to pass on this family mantle, as if she finally understood the pleasure her grandmothers must have felt when giving her the quilt tops many years earlier. DiAnn promised to take only one and give the other to her brother, with the added assurance that both quilts would eventually be passed along to grandchildren.

DiAnn chose the pastel Grandmother's Flower Garden for Mary Christina. The nineteen hexagons in each "flower" were perfectly hand stitched, without puckers or warped pieces. A double row of creamy white muslin hexagons surrounded each of the twenty-seven multi-colored flowers. The border was a sea green color, giving the quilt top a light, spring look.

When DiAnn asked me to quilt it, she didn't give any specific instructions. "Just make it look authentic," she admonished. The top was probably pieced in the 1930s, so I quilted it closely, following seam lines around each hexagon. I also did lots of quilting in the green border.

DiAnn picked up the finished quilt in time for the bridal shower. She told me afterward that the couple received scores of wonderful gifts, including china, crystal, silver, and kitchen appliances. "But," she said, "the quilt brought tears to many eyes when the box was opened."

DiAnn had written and embroidered a brief history of the quilt on a piece of fabric, then stitched it to the muslin backing. When the bride-to-be read the story about her great-great-grandmother's piecing this quilt, she realized the value of a multi-generational heritage. She vowed to keep the quilt in her family and one day to pass it along again.

The Quilting Frame: God loves marriage! In Malachi 2:15 God ordains the union of a man and a woman through this covenant promise of matrimony to each other. It is from such a commitment that godly offspring are brought into the world who will carry His purpose to the next generation. God loves life! A bridal shower is the perfect time to pass on a family heirloom, especially when it symbolizes covenant love that has been handed down through several generations.

God's Template: "But the plans of the LORD stand firm forever, the purposes of his heart through all generations" (Psalm 33:11).

The Binding Stitch: May the legacy of my life teach those who come after to trust in You and to enjoy the abundance of Your love.

Scrap Bag: Not interested in making a large quilt? Try something small! You can make calico Christmas gifts or party favors using diamonds, triangles, or hexagons, with a paper-piecing method. If you have time you can cut your own paper shapes, or you can buy them pre-cut at quilt shops. Look for instructions in books, magazines, and at quilt shows.

State Fair Quilters

If you go to the Minnesota State Fair, look for the Rosemore family in the Creative Arts Building. You'll have no trouble finding them—just go to the crowded booth filled with quilters.

Every year, Arlean Rosemore and about eighteen relatives put on matching T-shirts and staff a booth which incorporates hands-on participation and community involvement. Even Arlean's preschool grandchildren enjoy standing on an ice chest and explaining their work to passers-by.

One purpose of the Rosemore booth is to have fun. This family is well-known throughout central Minnesota as a cooperative quilting dynamo. Several of Arlean's grown children are award-winning quilters, and the grandchildren are already showing interest. The whole family once worked under a tight deadline to complete a quilt for the Minnesota Twins' baseball team, which they auctioned for charity. Another time, they made a quilt simulating a Monopoly™ game board, complete with play money. The state fair booth, like their other quilting projects, affords them time to enjoy one another's company.

A second purpose of the booth is to give children a taste of quilt-making. Each child who stops by is allowed to decorate a quilt block with fabric crayons. "The finished products look like refrigerator art," says Arlean. "We encourage them to draw something they did or saw at the fair that day." The youngest children—mere toddlers—join the fun by scribbling on a block. Older children draw on a block and help with the layout of the quilt top. After blocks are sewn together by one of the Rosemores, children help tie the layers together with yarn. At one recent fair, 242 youngsters participated.

Perhaps the booth's most significant purpose is the resulting bedcovers. Arlean says, "They are suitable for children to drag around for a security quilt." The Rosemores donate most of them to Ronald McDonald houses, but other good causes benefit as well. A few quilts are given to a local police officer, who keeps them in her squad car. When she has to remove children from dangerous situations, she wraps them in quilts, which they are allowed to keep. Other quilts are given to children in distressed areas across the globe, through Arlean's sister, a medical missionary. Last year the family sent forty-two quilts overseas.

It's a lot of effort, gathering supplies and manning a booth at the state fair, then putting together dozens of quilts they'll never see again. Why do the Rosemores do it, year after year?

Arlean explains, "All our little ones are safe and warm, but our hearts hurt when we think that there are so many babies who aren't." Through the years Arlean taught her family to think of others rather than live selfishly. "I always told them we ought to give back, because we have so much."

The Rosemores' quilts are one way they give back to the community. A simple bedcover with refrigerator art may not seem like a huge gift, but, Arlean says, it's worth it if "even one small quilt warms one small child."

The Quilting Frame: The Rosemores are a family bonded by a sense of purpose, and the time they spend together impacts others in a positive way. As Christians, we are born into the family of God. We experience deep relationships with others who are also called to common goals of loving service that glorifies His name and invites others to enjoy His grace.

God's Template: "And let us consider how we may spur one another on toward love and good deeds. Let us not give up meeting together, as some are in the habit of doing, but let us encourage one another—and all the more as you see the Day approaching" (Hebrews 10:24–25).

The Binding Stitch: Give us the grace to work cheerfully together and warm those in need.

Scrap Bag: Carpal tunnel syndrome sometimes affects the wrists of people who do repetitive work with their hands. Among its victims are musicians, computer operators, and quilters. See your doctor if you feel unusual discomfort in your quilting hand and wrist. You may need to reduce your daily quilting hours to avoid CTS. Or, like the Rosemores, teach your family how to quilt so you can get more done in less time.

Quilted Memories

After the death of Uncle Wayne, Linda's family was allowed to choose a few mementos for keepsakes. She and her husband looked through items collected and stored over many years, and they selected a dusty cedar chest in the basement. They promised to give it to their oldest daughter as a memory of her great-grandmother and her great-uncle Wayne.

They took it home and set it in a place of honor but didn't have time to look at the contents carefully until a few days later. "Inside," Linda says, "we found some games from Wayne's childhood and a few books. We also found a quilt!"

This quilt wasn't the standard calico print they might have expected to find in an antique trunk. Rather, it was made of heavy materials—wools, maybe from men's suits, and many other fabrics which can't be easily identified. The piecing pattern was a log cabin barn-raising, in which light and dark colors are alternated for an overall look of concentric diamonds. Light colors included pinks, greens, and a little beige, while the darks were black, navy, and brown. A red center in each block served to unify the log cabins. The backing contained a repeating pattern of a lake scene, whose fabric a quilt appraiser dated to the 1880s.

More unusual, though, was what accompanied the quilt. As Linda describes, "It had all kinds of tiny pieces of paper pinned to it. On the papers were names of people. There was also a larger paper saying, 'Made by Aunt Aleen before 1930.'" They recognized the handwriting of Wayne's mother, a meticulous record-keeper.

Linda and her husband couldn't identify any names except Aunt Aleen. Who were these people? Cousins? Neighbors? Quilting friends? And why were their names pinned to certain blocks in the quilt?

"We don't know the answers," Linda says, "but the quilt is special to us anyway." Eighty-six inches square, it hangs in their hallway, where they see it every day. "It's in gorgeous condition, so it probably wasn't used often." It may have had a place of honor, perhaps at the foot of a guest bed. Linda may never know who the people were, how they were involved with the quilt, or why the quilt is in such good condition after so many years. But she greatly appreciates the family significance and treasures the quilt as an heirloom.

The Quilting Frame: The mysteries of God can make life seem at times as though we are "looking through a darkened glass." We question why certain things are, or why others things are not, but God simply asks us to trust Him. There must be uncertainties for there to be a need for "trust," so these very mysteries may be present to draw us closer to God. It is in this closeness that we experience Him and find our faith has increased.

God's Template: Jesus said, "Do not let your hearts be troubled. Trust in God; trust also in me" (John 14:1).

The Binding Stitch: Lord, You said that we are blessed if we believe without seeing, so I trust my uncertainties to You, knowing that answers will come when they are needed to clear my path (John 20:29).

Scrap Bag: To keep quilts looking nice on the bed, refrain from tossing items onto them, such as purses, coats, school books, etc. Such things have dirt which can be transferred to the quilts. Also, sitting on the quilt while it's on the bed is not the best idea. It stretches the stitching, sometimes to the point of breaking.

The Quilt Jacket

When a couple of Missouri residents visited a department store near Escondido, California, they had no idea of the surprise awaiting them. Deen and Bob Weilder wandered through the women's clothing area, and Deen noticed a display of colorful garments—jackets, vests, skirts—all made from recycled quilts. At random, she pulled a jacket out, looked at it and immediately "got goosebumps all over."

That jacket had her mother-in-law's name embroidered on it.

She called Bob to her side and showed him. "When he read it," she remembers, "he, too, was stunned. However, not knowing what a friendship quilt was, he had no idea what he was seeing and just kept saying, 'Why that's Mom. . .that's Mother.'" The jacket featured several other embroidered names he recognized as well. All had been his mother's friends, and most were deceased by now.

Deen and Bob, in their excitement, attracted a small crowd. "I told the clerk this signature was Bob's mother's and she had been dead for eight years," says Deen. She went on to explain that all the names were of people who had lived in Missouri. The clerk then remembered hearing of a man from Texas buying old quilts at garage sales around the country. He sold them to a clothing company, which fashioned them into garments to distribute to department stores.

Deen recalls the moment vividly. "The people around us seemed to feel as though they had a sort of religious experience, saying things like, 'How could this happen?' and 'It's just too much, I can't believe it!' Bob and I definitely felt as if God were saying, 'Some things are just meant to be.' "

Deen bought the jacket, and after she and Bob returned to Missouri, they began investigating. They found one person, whose name was on the jacket, still living in the area, and they paid her a visit. The eighty-year-old woman recounted friendship clubs of central Missouri in the 1930s. One member of the club would be chosen to receive quilt blocks made by the others. Each participant pieced a block, signed her name on it, and then embroidered the name.

Ten years after the department store incident, Deen still attracts attention when she appears in public in Jefferson City wearing her quilt jacket. The faded friendship blocks bring a smile to many who remember a simpler era. And the sheer chance of Deen's finding that jacket brings a look of amazement to all who hear the story.

The Quilting Frame: It's interesting that the quilt was transformed into a jacket, but even more fascinating is the fact that it was lost and now is found. The story brings to mind the old familiar song "Amazing Grace, how sweet the sound, that saved a wretch like me. I once was lost, but now am found, was blind but now I see." The transformation of who we become through God's love is interesting, but to know that His grace brought us from being lost to being found is fascinating.

God's Template: "You see, at just the right time, when we were still powerless, Christ died for the ungodly. Very rarely will anyone die for a righteous man, though for a good man someone might possibly dare to die. But God demonstrates his own love for us in this: While we were still sinners, Christ died for us" (Romans 5:6–8).

The Binding Stitch: Lord, You have brought us into this place of grace [a place of undeserved privilege] and we confidently look forward to becoming all that You have in mind for us to be (Romans 5:2 TLB).

Scrap Bag: To extend the life of your quilt, protect the end which will be near the head of the bed. Cut a strip of muslin (or any scrap fabric) about twelve inches wide and as long as the width of your quilt. Fold the strip over the end of your quilt and baste it on. You'll be stitching through the quilt as well as through the muslin on front and back of quilt. After a season of using the quilt on the bed, remove the muslin and wash it. The quilt will have stayed clean of hand creams, facial oils, and other soiling agents.

The Touch of the Quilt

Imagine a quilt with zippers, buttons, pockets, lace, and rickrack. Its neon colors scream at you, and its wild prints make you dizzy. Perhaps it's too bold for your home decor, too intense for your guest bed.

But for a visually-impaired child, it's perfect.

Quilts from Caring Hands (QCH) in Corvallis, Oregon, heard about the need for such quilts, and their reaction was immediate. "Our hands were in the air, volunteering, almost before the question was completed!" says June Nielson, one of the members. This dedicated group of women has focused on charity work since 1990, making bedcovers for children at risk, including babies of teen mothers, those in foster care, and those suffering from abuse. A couple of years after they formed the group, they became involved with the visually impaired.

When making these quilts, QCH members deviate from standard cotton materials and choose fabrics according to texture and color only. Their quilts might contain silks, satins, fake fur, seersucker and wool. June says, "We use as many different textures as possible, so a blind child's fingers learn to refine the sense of touch. We use bright neon colors and blacks, whites, reds, yellows—colors with high contrast. Our print patterns are bold and gaudy. For a child with limited sight, these stimuli help work the eye muscles." Through quilts, children learn to explore their environment in a safe, non-threatening setting.

Some of the quilt tops feature rickrack and other embellishments, along with pockets to hold squeaky toys. The backings, in contrast, are solid colors. This allows the caregiver to turn the quilt over and place an object on it, inviting the child to focus his limited vision on that one thing.

Besides serving as teaching tools, the quilts also give blind infants something to occupy their minds. Sighted children, when awake, are constantly watching the world around them, but blind children don't have that option. If they have a quilt, though, their hands can explore it when they're alone in the crib or playpen.

The usefulness of these quilts goes beyond the child, affecting physical therapists and parents as well. Mary Reid, coordinator of vision services for Williamette Educational Service District in Salem, says the quilts speak of caring. "They tell parents and specialists that they're not alone. There are others who care and want to walk by their side. The blankets from QCH are a reminder of this caring.

"These women," she says, "are a gift from heaven." Thanks to them and their wild quilts, dozens of blind children in Oregon have a jump start on learning.

The Quilting Frame: If we have become blind to the activity of God in our lives, we may need to add texture to our faith. When intimate moments with God are only a testimony of years past, then it is time to pray for different ways deepen our relationship with Him. Traditional rituals and activities lose their impact when they become predictable. God wants to walk with us daily to meet the needs of others in bolder, more caring, people-oriented ways that say, "God loves you, and so do I." When this happens, you *feel* your faith again.

God's Template: "For this very reason, make every effort to add to your faith goodness; and to goodness, knowledge; and to knowledge, self-control; and to self-control, perseverance; and to perseverance, godliness;

and to godliness, brotherly kindness; and to brotherly kindness, love" (2 Peter 1:5–7).

The Binding Stitch: Lord, keep me from being idle and unfruitful and bring me into the full knowledge of Who You are.

Scrap Bag: When you're on vacation, make it a "quilt trip" too. Look in the phone book for quilting and fabric stores, and take a tour. Large cities, such as Dallas and Fort Worth, Texas, have dozens of shops. But even in small towns you may find a delightful, homey store tucked away near the court square. Buy unusual fabric from each store, as a souvenir of the trip.

Time Well Spent

I don't do appliqué—usually.

A cross-stitching professional in Texas commissioned me to make a quilt based on one of her patterns, two white geese on a dark blue background. The female goose wore a decorated straw hat, and the male sported a snappy bow tie. A simple design for cross-stitching, however, became complicated as I adapted it to a quilt. Each tiny block of the cross-stitch grid converted into one piece of the quilt, which resulted in thousands of half-inch squares. I pieced these by machine, forming the bodies of the geese. Next, I appliquéd them to the background by hand. That job alone took about fourteen hours—every minute of it eye-straining, finger-numbing, shoulder-aching work.

The quilt top was now ready to be layered with batting and

backing, then quilted. I showed it to my husband, and with one look he said, "This'll have to be done again."

Words like that can put a quilter in a tailspin.

"The background isn't big enough to accommodate the size of the geese," he explained. "You need more empty space. Like a painting in a frame, your subject shouldn't fill up the whole area. The viewer's eyes need someplace to rest." He put an arm around my shoulders. "That's just my opinion, honey. You'll have to decide what to do."

Panic and despair overwhelmed me as I wiped away tears. I looked at the quilt top objectively and realized he was right. The lights burned late that night as I undid hundreds of appliqué stitches.

The next day I bought a bigger piece of background fabric and tackled the appliqué once more. Remarkably, the second effort took less time, and the finished appearance was better than the first. I was thrilled when I layered the quilt and put it into the frame.

I hadn't enjoyed redoing the appliqué. But the opportunity taught me a lesson: The finished product is as valuable as the sum of the time spent developing it, and I must always keep in mind the larger picture. The end result? A charming twin-size wall hanging which is worth all the hours and energy put into it.

The woman who commissioned me to do the quilt was also pleased with the finished product. So pleased, in fact, that she displays it at crafters' markets and wholesale book shows across the country. Now, ten years later, I still don't do much appliqué work, but I *can* do it if necessary. Those extra hours weren't wasted, after all.

The Quilting Frame: The Old Testament prophet Jeremiah had a similar dilemma. He spent days dictating a lengthy work of prose to his secretary, Baruch. Through an indirect route, their manuscript landed in the hands of an unbelieving king, who cut it to pieces with a knife and burned it in his fireplace. All their efforts became ashes in a matter of minutes. Now, Jeremiah and Baruch had a choice to make: do the work again or sit and moan about their sorry situation. Without hesitation, they dipped their quills in the ink and unrolled a new scroll. The Bible states in Jeremiah 36:32 that they rewrote line after line, and this effort was even better than the first. Their finished product was more valuable than the extra time they'd spent on it.

God's Template: "Better is the end of a thing than the beginning thereof: and the patient in spirit is better than the proud in spirit" (Ecclesiastes 7:8 KJV).

The Binding Stitch: Lord, help me to remember that, even when I can't see the end of my work, there is a reward for those who endure.

Scrap Bag: Always keep a good quality seam ripper nearby. While piecing, appliquéing, or quilting, you may need to take out a few stitches and rework them. You'll do it with less grumbling if you have the right tool.

The Security Quilt

W hen all else fails, reach for a quilt. This is a lesson Christine learned after her husband's mother had a heart attack.

On New Year's Day, while Mrs. Tangvald visited in Christine's home, she experienced chest pains. An emergency trip to the hospital diagnosed the problem, and doctors restricted the woman's travel for six months. This prevented her from returning to her home in Norway. Under the circumstances, she agreed to stay in the United States. Several years earlier, she had lived in this country, so she wasn't a complete stranger to our language and customs. Christine and her husband made arrangements for her in a nearby assisted living facility.

"We put together household items for her," Christine explains. "I gave her some furniture which she had given me years earlier, things which should have made her feel at home." They outfitted the older woman with dishes, pots, pans, and other items essential for housekeeping.

Yet, something didn't quite seem right. Mrs. Tangvald couldn't settle into her new surroundings. The apartment was comfortable and safe, but it wasn't her home. She was thousands of miles from friends and from her social circle of support.

Christine and Roald did everything they could to ease the transition, but nothing proved effective until Christine spread a quilt on the bed. "It was a Wedding Ring, done in a soft cream color with wine and navy blue pieces," Christine describes. "I could see the quilt's importance in giving her comfort in her new surroundings. She just beamed when I brought it into the room."

Even though Mrs. Tangvald hadn't seen that particular bedcover before, the hominess of it gave her a sense of contentment and peace. Christine believes quilts can do this when other things fail. "Quilts have a long-term feeling of security," she declares, though she can't exactly say why that's true. In the case of this Double Wedding Ring, the effects were obvious.

The quilt had little sentimental value before this incident. It had been made by unknown hands and purchased at a department store. But, because of its importance in Mrs. Tangvald's life, it has become a part of their family history. "When she's through with it, we'll give it to a great-grandchild to bridge several generations."

Quilting Frame: Loving people seems to be second nature to quilters. Why else would they spend long, tedious hours piecing and quilting these beautiful works of art and then give them away? It must be love that binds the layers of fabric to give a quilt that "long-term feeling of security." Quilts, unlike blankets, are never thrown away. They are passed on to a new family, or transformed into a jacket or pillow, but not discarded. The Bible says, in 1 John 2:17 that, "The world and its desires pass away, but the man who does the will of God lives forever."

God's Template: "And so faith, hope, love abide [faith–conviction and belief respecting man's relation to God and divine things; hope–joyful and confident expectation of eternal salvation; love–true affection for God and man, growing out of God's love for and in us], these three; but the greatest of these is love" (1 Corinthians 13:13 AMPLIFIED).

The Binding Stitch: Thank You for loving me so much that You gave up Your only Son, Jesus, so that I could have an eternal security because I believe in Him (John 3:16).

Scrap Bag: If you drop your needle when quilting, stop at
once! Try to keep your body very still and consider
where the needle has fallen. Then, with the least
amount of moving possible, search in that one area.
Even better: Have a friend or family member search
for you. Use a magnet and a flashlight to look for the
needle. Don't resume your work until you find it.
Otherwise, a person later could sit on that needle or
step on it barefooted and incur great discomfort.

The Pineapple Quilt

Quilts contain little more than fabric and thread. They do not contain medicinal healing properties—at least nothing that can be analyzed in a lab.

But the power of quilts sometimes goes beyond the lab.

Susan Balter tells about her daughter's friend, who was diagnosed with lymphoma. The young man in his late twenties underwent a bone marrow transplant and chemotherapy, but the procedures failed to bring about the desired results. Instead, he seemed to face certain death within weeks. Susan says, "He was essentially bedridden, in too much pain to move. He had sores in his mouth from the chemotherapy and couldn't eat. His white count was so low that he was constantly in and out of the hospital with infections and pain."

Susan thought of an approach beyond the medical. "I dropped

everything and started a quilt for him," she states. The center of the quilt features a pineapple in a rainbow of colors, some with a Jewish theme in honor of the young man's father, a Holocaust survivor. The queen-size quilt has a wide white border, suitable for friends' messages and signatures.

Following three weeks of machine piecing and quilting during every spare moment, Susan completed the quilt. She sent it, along with permanent marking pens, to her daughter. A quilt-signing party was immediately organized, and dozens of people showed up to write notes of encouragement to their sick friend. The honoree himself was unable to attend, so a few from the party took the quilt to him at his parents' home.

Then a surprising thing happened. "He rallied that day," Susan says, "and while his prognosis is still poor, he is now receiving a new experimental drug. He remains alive one year later and has even been able to go out with his friends."

The improvement has been gradual. He still walks stiffly because one of his vertebrae had collapsed during the ordeal. He's not completely cured, but the change has been dramatic. No one expected such a remarkable turnaround. His parents called Susan to tell how touched they were and how happy this quilt had made their son. Susan and her daughter, both physicians, doubt any miraculous properties of the quilt, but they acknowledge its positive effects. "While I do not credit the quilt with his recovery,"

Susan notes, "I do believe it brought a great deal of happiness at a particularly grim time in the life of this young man."

The Quilting Frame: God can use small ingredients to make big miracles happen, fabric and thread to lift hope in the sick, five loaves and two fish to feed five thousand hungry people, and faith the size of a mustard seed to move a mountain. Shouldn't we give all that we have to God just to see what He might do with it?

God's Template: "And God is able to make all grace abound to you, so that in all things at all times, having all that you need, you will abound in every good work" (2 Corinthians 9:8).

The Binding Stitch: Thank You, Lord for being attentive to our prayers and being sure to answer.

Scrap Bag: Many rotary cutters are on the market today. Ask for advice at a fabric shop or quilt guild, and buy a cutter, a large transparent ruler, and a cutting mat.

These tools will save you hours of time, will result in neater, more accurate quilt pieces, and will reduce physical stress on your hands and wrists.

Work and Rewards

T wo hundred twenty-seven hours.

That's how long it can take to hand-quilt a prize-winning work of art.

When Mary, my client in Missouri, contacted me for another quilting job, I eagerly accepted. I'd been working for her for nearly a decade and enjoyed handling her bright, colorful quilt tops. Her appliqué work showed intricate, masterful skill, and the piecing was always flawless. Each of her designs was chosen to reflect some traditional aspect of the art but contained an added flair all her own.

This one was no exception. It was a Log Cabin pattern, with colors that sang together. Bright blues, golds, purples, and reds combined to dazzle the eye in apparent randomness. But upon closer inspection, I could see the colors had been carefully placed for maximum effect. What made this quilt top even more interesting was the variety of appliquéd flowers interspersed among the log cabin blocks. Violets, daisies, tulips, and others, with their smaller counterparts on the trailing vine in the border, gave the quilt top a stunning look.

Mary's instructions to me were simple: "Quilt anywhere it needs it; we like lots of quilting!" I began by marking a diamond cross-hatch pattern in the background of each flower. Then I layered and basted the top, batting, and backing which she provided, and stretched the layers onto my PVC frame. For more than three months I quilted an average of fourteen hours a week. Sometimes I worked as much as twenty-four hours in a week, though my back and shoulder would ache after hour eighteen, and my fingers stung from the jabbing of the needle. In other weeks I'd take a breather and quilt only eight or ten hours.

I finally bound the quilt, took a few snapshots for my records, and shipped the quilt to Mary. Soon, I received a check and a big thank-you from Missouri. Another satisfactory job was finished.

I hardly thought about the Log Cabin quilt again, because my attention turned to another client and another job. But, months later, a second letter arrived from Mary. This one announced that the quilt had been entered in a prestigious show and won numerous awards, including Best Bed Quilt, Best hand-quilting, and Best of Show.

That second category caught my eye. To receive such recognition was a thrill, and it will inspire me to continue to do my best work. When I look at my snapshots of Mary's Log Cabin quilt, I'll remember the 227 hours and the reward of work well done.

The Quilting Frame: Have you ever noticed how much easier a task is when your heart is in it? God's Word says, "Whatever you do, work at it with all your heart, as working for the Lord, not for men, since you know that you will receive an inheritance from the Lord as a reward. It is the Lord Christ you are serving" (Colossians 3:23–24). In context of the chapter, this refers to the job that we do for someone in authority. Hard work has a greater reward than just a paycheck.

God's Template: "His master replied, 'Well done, good and faithful servant! You have been faithful with a few things; I will put you in charge of many things. Come and share your master's happiness!' " (Matthew 25:21).

The Binding Stitch: Thank You, Lord, for giving me work that I can love, and for giving me love that works.

Scrap Bag: Always sign and date your quilt, even if you keep it for yourself. Use a permanent pen or write in pencil and then embroider it. Sign on the back or on the front, as an artist does on a painting. Make your signature as ornate as you want, adding flowers or other designs. Another choice is to sew a signature panel made of plain cotton fabric onto the quilt. You can sometimes buy such panels already printed on fabric, or you can purchase a book of iron-on stencils.

In Memory of Tamara

To endure a senseless, cruel tragedy is commendable; to turn that tragedy into a blessing for hundreds of others is remarkable.

Sharon Hanks has done both. Her fifteen-month-old daughter, Tamara, lost her life at the hands of a baby sitter. Sharon's earliest reactions involved anger, drugs, and thoughts of suicide. "But," she says, "I had so much to live for—three other children who depended on me, so I had to find a way to get through this."

The only way she could think of was prayer. "I dropped to my knees and asked God to take this and make it out for good." She also asked for strength to care for her surviving children.

That prayer was answered in many ways. Sharon found a support group for parents in Missouri. Through this, she's received love and care from others who have been through the same grief.

Next, she found a way to put her creative energies to work. "I make dolls, stuffed animals, doll clothes, and quilts for dolls and kids," she says. "I give them in Tamara's name to hospitals, shelters, churches, and other organizations for sick, abused, and homeless children." Her quilts are made of six-inch squares and triangles, all quick-pieced for service and durability. She incorporates a variety of colors, making her quilts look like Joseph's coat of biblical fame.

To keep her work going and her supply closet full, friends give Sharon fabric scraps, quilt batting, and other craft items. She also accepts unfinished crafting projects, which she "spices up" and uses in a variety of ways. Her three living children, now teens, get involved as well. "They seem to love this," she notices. "They're doing something in their sister's name to help others."

Life is now good for Sharon, who is married to a loving, supportive husband. "My family is my joy, my gift from God," she says. But she'll never forget Tamara. She'll continue to help ease the pain others may feel when faced with unthinkable circumstances. She'll continue to make quilts in Tamara's name.

The Quilting Frame: Throughout the history of God's people as given to us in the Bible, we see that life is a test. We have before us the option to trust God "no matter what," or to walk away from Him. To walk away from God is to leave the fragments of our dreams in pieces on the floor, but to trust Him is to let God pick up the pieces and make us whole again. When we choose to let Him make us whole again, He will make our lives more beautiful than before.

God's Template: "May God himself, the God of peace, sanctify you through and through. May your whole spirit, soul and body be kept blameless at the coming of our Lord Jesus Christ" (1 Thessalonians 5:23).

The Binding Stitch: Father in heaven, we know that You did not appoint us to suffer wrath but to receive salvation through our Lord Jesus Christ Who died for us so that, whether we are awake or asleep, we may live together with Him (1 Thessalonians 5:9–10).

Scrap Bag: Take a quilting class! Nearly every city has adult education classes offered at a high school or community college. Or, you can find a quilting class through your local fabric or crafts shop. You'll meet quilters, beginners and advanced, and you'll gain skills, insights, and friendships you would not find otherwise.

Giving for a Lasting Reward

How can you just give it away?"

That's what Jody White heard when she donated her hand-made quilt to the church's auction. The 2,277-piece Grandmother's Flower Garden required untold hours of cutting, piecing, and quilting, but Jody didn't mind. Giving it away may eventually result in something more valuable than the price of a quilt or the investment of her labor.

"I see people coming to know God because of this quilt," she explains. Each year Pines Baptist Church of Spokane, Washington, holds a huge auction to raise money for projects in their youth department. Until recently, the money was used to send dozens of teenagers to summer camp.

Last year, the youth group tried something different: a program called World Changers, which offers an opportunity to share God's love in a practical way. With the city's cooperation and blessing, the young people spend part of their summer renovating houses for low-income families. Fifteen Pines Baptist youth went last year to Bremerton, Washington, for example, joining two hundred others from across the country to renovate twenty-two houses. "It gets them actively involved in meeting the needs of the community," explains Jody. "When you see a teenager at sundown who says he can't get off the roof because he's not finished working, you know you've got some dedicated kids." As they work, they tell people why they've come. They explain that their love for God leads them to serve in this way.

Thanks to the auction and Jody's quilt, the teens have the funds to travel to needy communities again. This year's auction raised fifteen thousand dollars—more than enough to involve several youth in another World Changers project. Jody's quilt was only one of scores of items at the auction, but it was likely the most memorable. It's queen size, and the colors are a scrap-bag mix, selected from Jody's own collection of fabrics. When people see it, they're awed by the handwork and by Jody's willingness to part with it. But she says, "It's no problem giving it to the auction. This is the way I can use my quilting talents for the greatest good."

Quilting Frame: Jody uses her unique abilities to gain
wealth that can be shared with others, and thus posi-
tions herself to receive abundant returns from God.
Matthew 25 tells the parable of the man who,
like God, entrusted his wealth to his servants.
Depending on the unique abilities of the workers, he
gave them various amounts of money to invest while
he was away. The first two workers traded wisely and
doubled their portions. The last servant foolishly hid
both his money and his ability to gain wealth, then
blamed his laziness on his fear that he wouldn't have
the money to give back to the master upon his return.
The master was angry at his idleness and told him to
give what talent he had to the other servant who knew
what to do with it.

God's Template: "For everyone who has will be given more,
and he will have an abundance. Whoever does not
have, even what he has will be taken from him"
(Matthew 25:29).

*The Binding Stitch: Father, thank You for giving me unique
abilities to invest in the lives of others. I know You will give
back to me more than I give away.*

Scrap Bag: I baste my quilt layers with inexpensive thread. It's only used for a short time; then it's removed and thrown away. Sometimes I find it on sale in a craft store, and I purchase several colors. I don't, however, baste with red thread. It can leave a telltale hint of red color on light fabrics, even after it's removed.

Mystery Book

I just can't figure it out.

The package arrived, bearing only the return address of a bookstore. No card or note inside—nothing to tell me who sent it. Maybe someday I'll learn the identity of the benefactor. Meanwhile, I'll enjoy it and add it to my growing quilt library.

This library began with an inexpensive how-to book, purchased decades ago, when I was a quilting novice. From it I got the inspiration to make a postage-stamp quilt, piecing row upon row of small squares of calico.

Next, my husband bought me a book of Early American quilt patterns, from which I learned to piece small triangles. I made a Bear's Paw quilt for our bed, using autumn colors, and I made a Turkey Tracks Quilt for my sister's anniversary, with bright reds and muslin.

Then I found a paperback collection of quilting designs. That book taught me how to use a thimble correctly and how to make tiny, even stitches. I also learned that quilting doesn't have to be simple straight lines. It can be ornate and decorative as well as functional. I've traced the quilting lines from that book onto many quilt tops.

Another addition to my library was a book of friendship quilts. It gave me ideas for three signature patterns. My first was a brown-and-green triangle design interspersed with names of South Carolina friends. Second was the family album quilt, where names decorate panels between dark-print pinwheels. The third was my red, white, and blue Texas quilt, whose signatures complement small and large log cabin blocks.

Last Christmas I received a book of Japanese quilt patterns, containing exotic names such as ikegaki, matsuri, and funade. I made the hikidashi (decorative box) pattern into a wall hanging using some authentic Asian fabrics. It serves as a distinct contrast to my American quilts.

Each quilt book I own has encouraged me, inspired me, and furthered my skills as a quilter. Sometimes I reread portions of a book, to review a procedure I used long ago. Occasionally, I see a word of instruction which points to a flaw in my quilting or piecing methods. When that happens, I make adjustments.

And now I have the mystery book. It's a collection of diary

entries, written by a woman who quilts professionally—a great source of inspiration. The colorful photographs and interesting text keep me reading and enjoying the book. As I read, I'll probably come across something that I can incorporate into my quilting life.

The individual who sent it knows me well enough to give me something I can use and enjoy. In return, I will read it and thus say thanks to the mysterious giver!

The Quilting Frame: Like the mystery book that arrived in my mail, the Bible may puzzle us. When we first open it, we don't know the One who sent it to us, or how He knew we would both enjoy and need it. And like the instructions in my quilting books, the Bible's message must be *read* and put into practice. As we use what we learn from God's Word, our faith is perfected and the work of our hands becomes a masterpiece that others can enjoy, too.

God's Template: "Anyone who lives on milk, being still an infant, is not acquainted with the teaching about righteousness. But solid food is for the mature, who by constant use have trained themselves to distinguish good from evil" (Hebrews 5:13–14).

The Binding Stitch: I fix my eyes on You, Jesus, the author and perfecter of my faith (Hebrews 12:2).

Scrap Bag: If you can't find a local quilt class, watch television! Many of the cable channels now have home shows which feature quilting. You'll also find quilt instruction on public television. Check your local television listings.

The Quilt that Healed

Sometimes, when helping someone else, a person discovers she has helped herself as well.

Joanne Palik of Toronto, Canada, is a good example. After a difficult childhood, she was left at age sixteen with the responsibility of caring for her invalid mother, who would live bedridden another twelve years. As the older woman lay dying, she could not speak, but she mouthed the words to Joanne, "Don't ever lose your kind heart." That sentence sustained Joanne through her initial grief.

Coincidentally, the parents of Joanne's close friend died within the next three years. As Joanne recalls, the friend was "so loved by her parents that I could only imagine the pain she was in. I felt so much grief for this woman. She was so spiritual, and here I felt helpless."

Joanne had recently learned to quilt. One day, while in her sewing room, she thought of the friend. "I remember looking up and saying, 'Please help me lessen her pain.' " Even though Joanne had never heard of a memory quilt, the idea of one came "rushing through me with such urgency." She immediately drafted a plan.

Through the years, Joanne had collected used clothing to give to needy people, so it was not surprising when she approached the friend with a request to donate some of her parents' clothes. The friend had no objections, lovingly offering Joanne several items from her mother's and father's wardrobes. She also included good bed linens.

Joanne's next step involved hours in the sewing room, sorting, cutting, marking, and making notes. Then, a phone call went to the friend's daughter, asking secretly to borrow family photos. "With a transfer medium I imported photographs such as her parents' wedding picture, family group shots, and others, onto the fabrics," says Joanne.

Her pattern was the famous Dresden Plate. Joanne transferred more than twenty family pictures onto the "plates," with the wedding picture in the middle of one of them. The overall color scheme was red and pink, to match the mother's bedroom design. The blocks were made from a favorite hunting shirt, a favorite blouse, and assorted housecoats, shirts, and pants. The quilt's backing was one of the parents' bedsheets.

More than a year after the inspirational beginning, the memory quilt was finished. Joanne presented it as a birthday gift to her friend. "She was so stunned she couldn't speak for a very long time," Joanne remembers. "We sat in silence with no words between us."

Mixed in with the emotions of joy and sorrow, Joanne felt something more. "That is when I realized I did my own healing towards the death of my mother while trying to tell my friend that I understood the pain of losing her parents. The quilt helped her more than empty words, and it helped me, too."

The Quilting Frame: In times of hardship, great comfort comes from those who can offer empathy and hope for better days in the future. The Bible says in Hebrews 2 that Jesus can empathize with us because He was tempted in every way, just as we are; yet because He remained without sin He is able to stand before God and ask for help on our behalf, so that we can "approach the throne of grace with confidence, so that we may receive mercy and find grace to help us in our time of need" (Hebrews 4:16).

God's Template: "Praise be to the God and Father of our Lord Jesus Christ, the Father of compassion and the God of all comfort, who comforts us in all our troubles, so that we can comfort those in any trouble with the comfort we ourselves have received from God." (2 Corinthians 1:3–4).

The Binding Stitch: Your unfailing love comforts me. Show me ways to share Your love with those who need to be consoled (Psalm 119:76).

Scrap Bag: Don't like to baste with needle and thread? You might try safety pins. Or, you can buy a punching machine, which will punch and secure your layers with a thin strand of plastic, similar to the method of attaching price tags to clothing in department stores. After the quilt is finished, clip the strands with sharp scissors.

Grandma's Quilt

The Churn Dash quilt pattern originated in the early part of the nineteenth century.

I have a Churn Dash quilt originating in the early part of the twentieth century, but it almost didn't make it into the twenty-first.

In the first decade of the 1900s, my mother was born. Her mother was a first-grade teacher, who also taught piano and quilted in her free time. Grandma's quilts were not showpieces but practical, everyday bedcovers, made for a lifetime of service for her growing family. Her quilts were usually scrappy affairs, whose colors often mixed and mismatched. They had a unifying background color, though, so her quilts always seemed well planned.

The Churn Dash was one of her earliest efforts. A variation of the nine-patch block, a Churn Dash pattern incorporates triangles and squares. In most quilt books illustrating churn dashes, the triangles are one color, the squares are another, and the background is neutral.

Grandma must have worked hard to make the color combinations pleasing to the eye. Most—but not all—of her squares complement the triangles. Her background, rather than neutral beige or white muslin, is bright yellow.

As a child, I loved that quilt. It came to our house after Grandma's death in 1963, and I slept under it for years. I never tired of looking at the tiny prints, wondering why Grandma chose a certain color when piecing a certain block.

In the late 1960s we had a near tragedy involving this quilt.

I must have become too warm one night while sleeping, and I pushed off some of the covers, including the Churn Dash quilt. Its edge slipped into my baseboard electric heater, where it rested for several hours. In the morning we discovered the quilt, partially blackened and smoldering on the floor beside my bed.

Thankfully, the quilt didn't ignite into a blaze. It didn't catch my sheets or curtains on fire. It didn't fill the house with smoke or cause any other damage. It didn't even singe the floor! As we—Dad, Mother, Linda, and I—stood in my room that morning, we were struck with a sense of awe in God's watchcare over us.

Afterwards, Mother and I repaired the Churn Dash quilt, though it didn't look exactly as it did when Grandma Lowry made it. Still,

I treasure it even more, thinking of what might have happened that night. I now have plans to make a replica of this special quilt. I bought bright yellow fabric for the background, and I'm collecting tiny prints to mix and mismatch the triangles and squares.

The Quilting Frame: Sometimes our earliest efforts of walking with God seem awkwardly filled with actions mismatched to our goals. Pieces of our old life may not complement the new work God is doing in us, but the redemptive process will eventually transform us to be like Him. We may not realize what a good work He has done in us until we are tested by the fires of life, but like Grandma's quilt on the heater, we will find protection and safety as we trust Him.

God's Template: "Being confident of this very thing, that He who has begun a good work in you will complete it until the day of Jesus Christ" (Philippians 1:6 NKJV).

The Binding Stitch: Thank You Lord, for giving Your angels charge over me to accompany and defend and preserve me in all of my ways (Psalm 91:11).

Scrap Bag: If you have trouble keeping up with your scissors while quilting, consider putting them on a string. A small pair of scissors can be hung at your waist or around your neck when you're sitting at the quilt frame. (Caution: For safety's sake, don't walk around with scissors on your body. An accidental fall could result in serious injury.) In Victorian days, women wore chatelaines, or decorative bands of fabric which were suspended from the waist. Chatelaines held keys, scissors, and other necessities.

Quilts with a Purpose

Not every quilt has a beautiful, homey message of family and love; some have a different purpose. They may serve to educate, make a political statement, or promote awareness of a sensitive issue. Quilt artist Rosanna Lynne Welter's piece, "A Rose for Pain," does all of this.

"I am especially concerned," says the West Valley City, Utah, resident, "with the welfare of animals in cities and how they are abandoned to fend for themselves when they have no skills to do so. Many of these animals live very brief lives filled with hunger, pain, and suffering."

While considering this senseless cruelty some time ago, she remembers, "I saw an image of a fish, segmented in alternating pieces between its flesh and its bones." The graphic mental picture stayed with her for two years, while she learned to dye her own fabrics and make phototransfers onto cloth. Finally, she was ready to put the quilt together. Silky yellow and pink roses are interspersed among stark pictures of various animals, all having only partial bodies of flesh and the rest skeleton.

In 1998, she entered the quilt in *Quilter's Newsletter Magazine*'s "Rhapsody of Roses" international competition, and the judges were impressed. As a contest finalist, the quilt toured the globe, stopping for exhibitions in such places as Innsbruck, Austria; Lyon, France; and Houston, Texas.

Rosanna knows the quilt isn't pleasant viewing for traditional quilt lovers. She admits it's her first work to address an issue rather than simply trying to be pretty. "Although many people find it disturbing," she explains, "I think it speaks the truth, and I hope it inspires people to be more caring and respectful of animals."

If the quilt can educate and inspire its viewers to a greater concern for animals, then Rosanna's goal will be reached. "I hope it grabs people and changes them, makes them think, gets them involved."

The Quilting Frame: Like the contrast of Rosanna's quilt,
our choices will lead to life or death. Deuteronomy

30:19–20 tells of the time God spread the options before His people saying, "I call heaven and earth as witnesses against you that I have set before you life and death, blessings and curses. Now choose life, so that you and your children may live and that you may love the LORD your God, listen to his voice, and hold fast to him. For the LORD is your life, and he will give you many years in the land he swore to give to your fathers, Abraham, Isaac and Jacob."

God's Template: "The creation waits in eager expectation for the sons of God to be revealed" (Romans 8:19).

The Binding Stitch: Lord, show me the ways that gratify You, so that the fruit of my work will build up and not destroy the work of Your hands.

Scrap bag: Try designing your own quilt block on graph paper. Simply alternating two traditional blocks, such as bear's paw and nine-patch, without sashing between the blocks gives the quilt top a contemporary, geometric look. A variety of quilt-design programs are available on the Internet, at your local quilt shop, and through advertisements in quilt magazines.

Therapy Quilts

A functional quilt frame can be a symbol of fellowship, says Christine Tangvald. She remembers her mother's frame. "It was a big thing that could be taken apart and set up anywhere." Once a month, it was hauled out of storage and taken to someone's home for a quilting bee.

Six to eight women gathered for each bee. The hostess had lunch in the oven and enough fabric for several quilts.

"You understand, they didn't make fancy pieced quilts, with ornate quilting," Christine points out. No, these bedcovers would be strictly utilitarian. Tops and backings were always large pieces of fabric, and batting came from local materials, like wool from her grandfather's flock of sheep, Christine remembers.

Work at the bee began with an animated discussion of which

plaid, print, or stripe was appropriate for matching or contrasting the top with the backing. After coming to an agreement, they stretched a backing onto the big frame, tacking it to the wood. Next, a batt was cut to size and laid on the backing. Finally, the top was stretched onto the batt, and the textile sandwich was ready to tie together.

Using a large darning needle threaded with yarn, a woman took one stitch down through the three layers, then up, making that stitch as small as possible. Then she took another small stitch about four inches away, working right to left. Continuing in this manner, several women in tandem soon had the quilt secured. From the backing, one could see a pattern of small stitches in neat rows, evenly spaced. A view from the top exposed the stretches of yarn between the small stitches.

But soon sharp scissors clipped the lengths of yarn halfway between every two stitches, and fast fingers tied them to their own tails. The result was a functional tied quilt, ready to be finished with a machine binding.

Christine remembers getting special permission to ride the school bus to this house with other children whose mothers attended the bee. After milk and cookies many of the boys and girls ran out to play. But Christine preferred to stay indoors. The women gave her the special task of standing under the quilt frame while they worked. She took the underside stitch and pushed the needle back up through the quilt, working in rhythm with one of the quilters. To a six-year-old girl, the thrill of quilting with adults would be long treasured.

Throughout the process, conversation abounded. Christine believes the camaraderie was more valuable than the quilts themselves. "Women could talk recipes, flu, child-rearing, pregnancies, and so forth. It was a great bonding time for them." Many problems were solved around the quilting frame, as women asked advice or poured out their troubles. The quilt-making process was special not only for the resulting quilts, but for the friendships that were nurtured as well.

"I called them Therapy Quilts," says Christine. "They were the therapy that kept our community of Lamont, Washington, going."

The Quilting Frame: Fellowship is one blessing of our faith. Because we know that God loves us, we have courage to love others, and love is the thread which holds our collective works together for the benefit of all. It is when this love unites us into one body, working together, that we see both the beauty and the utilitarian virtues of our faith.

God's Template: "By this all men will know that you are my disciples, if you love one another" (John 13:35).

The Binding Stitch: "Let my teaching fall like rain and my words descend like dew, like showers on new grass, like abundant rain on tender plants" (Deuteronomy 32:2).

Scrap Bag: A large room is needed for a traditional quilting frame, which is usually wooden, with two poles longer than the width of a quilt. The backing, batting, and top are layered and basted, then rolled onto the poles, much like a window shade on a roller. The poles are set into the stand and quilting begins. The smaller, modern PVC frames don't need a large room. The layered and basted quilt is simply laid onto the top of the frame, and clamps secure the fabric onto the PVC pipes.

A Quilt like Grandmother's

Making a quilt can serve as therapy for a troubled soul.

Imagine these situations: enduring an ugly divorce, losing custody of your only child, watching the father take her far away, struggling to pay attorney bills, being attacked and almost raped, surviving breast cancer. Each of these sounds terrible, but a woman having to face them all must look for a strength greater than herself.

Such was the case of Shirlene, whose name has been changed here for privacy. "Through it all," she says, "I knew the hand of God was upon me." She also knew she needed a purposeful activity, so she decided to try quilting. Her project would be patterned after her grandmother's Double Wedding Ring quilt, which she remembered as a child. It would offer something constructive to fill her days. It would help take her mind off the traumatic events. Best of all, she says, it would be something to give to her daughter "so that she would know that her mother and mother's family loved her and always will."

At the time, Shirlene didn't know anyone who quilted. She couldn't even find books or magazines on the subject, so she tried it on her own. Determined to make the quilt entirely by hand, she used trial and error to get the job done. At times her methods were unorthodox. She didn't know how to choose fabrics, for example. Some in her quilt are cotton; some are cotton/polyester. "One piece," she admits, "even has some plastic flower petals on it."

She didn't know how to hide knots when quilting, either. So, whenever she needed to start a new length of thread, she'd take the quilt off the hoop and separate the layers of an unquilted section. Then she'd draw the threaded needle between layers and up through the top to begin quilting again.

Fortunately, Shirlene regained custody of her daughter, and during the following years the child—and then the young woman—watched the quilt grow as her mother had time to work on it. It was completed when this daughter became a mother herself.

Now, Shirlene looks back on those terrible events and sees that the comfort of God and the comfort of a quilt like grandmother's helped pull her through.

The Quilting Frame: Quilting offered Shirlene a valuable
lesson in patience. Just as a quilt is not finished until its
raw edges are bound, she learned that her testimony of
trials was not complete until her heart was victoriously
bound to God through His grace. Grace says, "Come to
me, all you who are weary and burdened, and I will
give you rest" (Matthew 11:28). Our only action is to
persevere in trust until God fulfills His promise to work
things out on our behalf. Hope and patience will see us
through to the day when all of our "raw edges" are
neatly bound into the love of God.

God's Template: "I say to myself, 'The LORD is my portion; therefore I will wait for him.' The LORD is good
to those whose hope is in him, to the one who seeks
him; it is good to wait quietly for the salvation of the
LORD" (Lamentations 3:24–26).

*The Binding Stitch: "I was wearied by all my ways, but I would
not say, 'It is hopeless.' I found renewal of my strength in
You Lord, and so I did not faint"* (Isaiah 57:10, author's
paraphrase).

Scrap Bag: If your quilt or your fabric stash receives smoke damage from a fire, do not wash in regular laundry detergent, which may set the smoky smell into the cloth. Rather, consult a professional cleaner for a special chemical solution to remove smoke.

Cousin Bevie

Always a smile on her face, I can still hear Bevie laugh today, and it makes me smile."

That's how Laura Hahn describes her cousin. Bevie was a creative person with many talents, and she had a way of getting things done and encouraging others to do the same. She was an excellent teacher and amazingly patient when instructing others. Quilting ranked high among Bevie's skills.

Their grandmother had given Bevie her quilting patterns, and Bevie chose one of them for a friendship quilt in 1960. During the next thirty-six years she made sailboat blocks and had friends sign them. As in-laws, children, and grandchildren were added to the family, she made blocks for them to sign, too. She embroidered the signatures when time allowed.

"Each block was put away in a special box she had been carrying around with her all those years," Laura remembers.

Sadly, Bevie's health suddenly deteriorated and she died within a few months. Now Laura was asked to go through Bevie's things. She found fabrics, templates, some blocks belonging to Grandma, two unfinished quilts, and the collection of sailboat blocks.

"I felt love as I touched these things," Laura recalls. She took them home and finished one of the quilts—a Log Cabin, giving it to Bevie's husband. The other unfinished quilt she plans to complete for Bevie's daughter.

"But the box of sailboat blocks is my link to Bevie. There were so many blocks, that I have made one quilt and still have enough to make another." Laura feels a strong connection to her cousin as she works on the quilts, and she wants to finish them as a legacy to her, in memory of Bevie's talents, patience, and smile.

The Quilting Frame: Bevie's creative way of sharing with others and expressing her love for people by adding them to her "special box" of quilt squares has eternal value. She reminds us that the only things we really leave behind us are the fruits of a life lived to glorify

God, and all we take with us is our love for God and others.

God's Template: "I will sing of the LORD'S great love forever; with my mouth I will make your faithfulness known through all generations" (Psalm 89:1).

Binding Stitch: Lord, may Your presence in my life keep my "special box" filled with love, joy, peace, patience, kindness, goodness, and faith.

Scrap Bag: How much fabric do you need to make a full-size quilt? It depends on the sizes and shapes of your individual pieces; dust off your junior high math skills and figure it out. Be sure to account for seam allowances when making the calculations. You may also want to check at a quilt shop for books on the subject.

New Lease on Life

When Peggy Gorsh's health problems became so severe that she couldn't continue her nursing career, she turned to quilting to fill the gap.

Peggy's medical history stems from a serious car accident at age fifteen. The resulting problems caused chronic pain, but she managed to enjoy life nonetheless, working for more than twenty-five years as a critical care nurse.

In her nursing role, she found pleasure in caring for others. "I had my life and career all figured out," she says. "Even after retirement, I would continue in home health care. I would do nursing until death took me."

But, Peggy's pain increased over the years, and she needed medication to endure. "I got epidurals and corticosteroid injections in the radiology department, then went right to my twelve- to eighteen-hour shift," Peggy recalls. "The pain was often so bad I slept at the hospital, because I hurt too much to walk to the parking lot."

By 1996, the injections had lost their effectiveness, forcing Peggy to make the most difficult decision of her life. She stepped down from the career she loved. She recalls, "I found myself in a role reversal. No longer a caregiver, now I needed caring for. I hated it!" She remembers this as a low point in her life. "I gained fifty pounds and sank into a depression so black I thought I would never climb out. I had always worked. I had no idea what to do with my time." Peggy believes that having nothing to contribute to society is a heartwrenching feeling. She says, "I began a downward spiral that only my supportive husband and a loving God could stop."

A surprising upturn occurred when a neighbor invited her to a meeting with the Iowa County Heartland Quilters. Her family saw this as a new avenue for Peggy and lent their support. "My husband," she says, "started planning trips to quilt stores and helped me shop. My daughter got me on the Internet," where she met dozens of quilting friends across the country. She learned of charity opportunities and began quilting for local hospice programs.

Peggy now quilts full time for charities and sews for her seven grandchildren. "Once I thought I would be a nurse until I died. Now I know God had another path chosen for me. My husband told me, 'When God gives you gifts, take them.' I plan not to argue."

While the handstitching that Peggy loves will never take the place of caring for her patients, it's the next best thing, she believes. That, and hugs from those grandchildren.

The Quilting Frame: The pain and hardships of life often cause us to work harder in order to deserve a good life filled with God's love. But God gives undeserved favor and spiritual blessings to those who put their hope in Christ so that we can be rescued from hardship. This unmerited divine assistance which is given to us for regeneration or sanctification is called "grace." It cannot be earned; therefore, work does not improve our right to receive it. In spite of grace, people are driven to the point of weariness trying to do great things for God, but all He wants is for us to enjoy His greatness.

God's Template: "For it is by grace you have been saved, through faith—and this not from yourselves, it is the gift of God—not by works, so that no one can boast. For we are God's workmanship, created in Christ

Jesus to do good works, which God prepared in advance for us to do" (Ephesians 2:8–10).

The Binding Stitch: Lord, thank You for loving me, not because of the good work I do; but because You love me, the work I do is good.

Scrap Bag: Want to make a business out of quilting? Many people earn a respectable income as full-time quilters. Before you begin, though, do some research on home businesses and quilt-related businesses in particular. Ask at the library or bookstore, and you'll find several good books on the subject.

Mother's Last Conversation

The final conversation I had with my mother was about quilts.

Of course, I didn't realize at the time that this would be our last interaction. I only knew that Mother was having a problem with her memory. Today we know the problem as Alzheimer's disease.

It began years earlier, when Mother called my sister and asked, "How do you multiply?" while filing her income tax returns. A series of blunders and confused situations followed, scenarios which all families of Alzheimer's victims would recognize—cooking at 2 A.M., forgetting to put on shoes before walking in the snow, and not recognizing close family members.

The situation worsened as years passed. Finally, Dad became ill with pneumonia and had to stay in bed. Mother cared for him briefly but became confused about his identity. A neighbor happened to drop by and immediately suspected a problem.

"You better stay outside," Mother cautioned. "Gramma's in the bed and she's really sick." The kind neighbor convinced her to open the door and quickly arranged for Dad to go to the hospital. Mother had to stay in a nursing home while Dad recovered.

I arrived to meet my sisters, Linda and Jean, and sister-in-law Pat, all of us from homes in other states. After determining that Dad was doing well, we went to see Mother in the nursing home.

She looked at us as if we were strangers but greeted us amiably. She invited us to sit in the lobby, and we settled ourselves on sofas and chairs. Each of us, in turn, tried chatting with her about subjects she might enjoy—weather, gardening, cooking. After several minutes of idle talk, the conversation ceased. Then, Mother shifted in her chair. Her hazel eyes brightened, and she turned to me with renewed interest, looking at me as if I'd just entered the room.

"And what kind of quilts are you working on these days?"

The question caught us all by surprise. As if a shaft of sunlight had peeked through the clouds, the atmosphere changed. Mother focused on me, and we had a real conversation. I told her about my Bear's Paw and my Turkey Tracks, and she reminisced about her most recent quilts. We laughed and discussed sewing machines, appliqué, thimbles—anything related to quilting.

Then the light went out. The hazel eyes dimmed, and as quickly as it had opened, the window of recognition closed. In the six years that followed, I visited Mother in the nursing home many times, but she didn't know me again.

Those few moments have remained a bright spot in an otherwise difficult period. Losing one's mother is not easy, but losing her slowly to a cruel, untreatable disease is even more difficult. I'm thankful to have had that final conversation with her, and I'm thankful it was centered around the hobby that gave us both such pleasure.

The Quilting Frame: King David found that good memories help us through times of trouble. He wrote: "When I was in distress, I sought the Lord; . . . I thought about the former days, the years of long ago; I remembered my songs in the night. . . . I will remember the deeds of the LORD; yes, I will remember your miracles of long ago. I will meditate on all your works and consider all your mighty deeds" (from Psalm 77).

God's Template: " 'Though the mountains be shaken and the hills be removed, yet my unfailing love for you will not be shaken nor my covenant of peace be removed,' says the LORD, who has compassion on you" (Isaiah 54:10).

The Binding Stitch: Lord, You are my refuge in times of oppression, my stronghold in times of trouble (Psalm 9:9).

Scrap Bag: Always have a small, portable project ready to carry with you at a moment's notice. I have a work-in-progress in its own bag, complete with needles, thread, scissors, and thimble. Whenever I go to sit with a friend in the hospital or wait at the airport for someone, I grab this bag.

Fun and Fellowship

Looking for a cute game for a quilters' meeting or a baby or bridal shower? Cut and distribute to all participants a small sample of each fabric, which will serve as answers to the following questions:

1. What's seen in the newspaper? (print material)
2. Who's a former leader of Russia? (linen)
3. What's as good as money? (check material)
4. What's used by a fisherman? (net)
5. Name two letters of the alphabet. (piqué)
6. How is a chair used? (satin)
7. What's worn in your shoes? (lace material)
8. What's a prophet and one who plays the stock market? (seersucker)
9. What should you take on an outdoor vacation? (outing flannel)
10. What sound is associated with a clock? (ticking)
11. What's seen in an American flag? (star prints or striped fabric)
12. What's the color of royalty? (purple material)

You may think of additional questions to suit your particular party. The simpler questions could be used at a children's party.

Additional Tips

List of resources for quilters:

Quilts from Caring Hands (from the story "The Touch of a
   Quilt")

www.reese.org/qch
or, write to them at
Quilts from Caring Hands
PMB 157
2397 NW Kings Blvd.
Corvallis, OR 97330

Sunshine Quilt Project (from the story "Warmth around the
   World")

www.hickoryhillquilts.com/goodworks.htm
or, http://sunshineguild.hypermart.net
or, phone Billijean Hobson toll-free at 1-877-731-5464
or, write to her at
Sunshine Quilts
415 Center Street
Pittsburgh, PA 15221

Child Abuse Quilts (from the story "Words Have Power")
www.members.tripod.com/mbgoodman/caqpics/caqindex.html

The Red Barn Quilting & Tea Room (from the story "The Hug Quilt")
E-mail Dale Potter at dpquilts@telusplanet.net

To see some of Sharon Hanks's projects (from the story "In Memory of Tamara"), contact her at cheripie@hotmail.com

Lessons on computer/photo transfer onto fabrics (from the stories "The Church Quilt" and "The Quilt that Healed")
http://quilting.about.com/hobbies/quilting/library/weekly/aa101199htm

Healing Hearts (from the story "Nelanna's Quilt")
http://albums.photopoint.com/i/AlbumIndex?u=30678Sa=1766961

Animal Abuse Quilts (from the story "Quilts with a Purpose")
http://rosanna.welter.home.att.net
www.arkonline.com
www.hsus.org

About the Authors

Ruth McHaney Danner of Spokane, Washington, has quilted for thirty years. She teaches quilting techniques in schools, children's clubs, craft shops, adult education classes, and quilt guilds. She is a member of the Washington State Quilters.

Ruth holds a BA in English from Harding University, Searcy, Arkansas; and an MA in religious education from Southwestern Baptist Theological Seminary, Fort Worth, Texas. She has taught school in Arkansas, Connecticut, South Carolina, Texas, and Washington. In addition, she serves in her church as pianist and Sunday school teacher.

She is also a freelance writer. Her articles have appeared in religious and family magazines, craft magazines, writers' periodicals, and newspapers. She is a member of a local writers' group as well as the National League of American Pen Women. This is her first book.

Contact Ruth McHaney Danner at
P.O. Box 18425
Spokane, WA 99228–0425
www.ipeg.com/~mdanner/quilting.htm

Cristine **Bolley** is the series editor for the new line of special interest devotionals from Promise Press. Her mission is to explain, exemplify, and establish the truth of God's power and the grace of His love with clarity. She inspires people to trust God for His purpose, plan, provision, and power to enjoy the abundant life His good news proclaims. Being well-traveled and having lived in Mexico and New Zealand, Cristine feels a passion for the global task of reaching people for Jesus Christ.

For three decades, she has worked with international ministries, including twenty years as an acquisition editor for Christian publishers. She is also a mother of three daughters who play volleyball, and best friend to James, her husband of nearly thirty years. When time allows she drinks tea with friends, watches wild birds at her feeders, makes scrapbooks, or browses antique shops for rare, yet affordable treasures.

In the last few years, Cristine has ghostwritten seven titles, and co-authored the devotional titled *When Every Hour's a Rush Hour,* which inspired mothers with guilt-busters, love-boosters, and time-savers for their busy families. She is now working on its sequel,

Time Out for Love, for busy wives, with her co-author Joann Webster. Her first illustrated children's book will be released in the fall of 2001, titled *A Gift from St. Nicholas.*

Contact Cristine Bolley at
Wings Unlimited
P.O. Box 691532
Tulsa, OK 74169–1532